Picnics, Potlucks & BBQs

Great Recipes

Printed in the United States of America
by G&R Publishing Co.

Distributed By:

 Products

507 Industrial Street
Waverly, IA 50677

ISBN-13: 978-1-56383-258-1
ISBN-10: 1-56383-258-5
Item #7022

Table of Contents

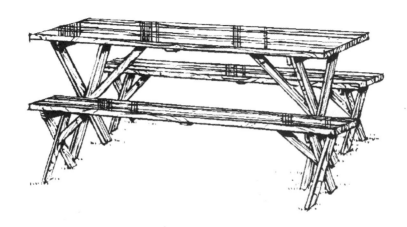

Good times call for great foods!

The next time you're invited to a picnic, potluck or barbecue, don't fret over what you should take to share. This cookbook is filled with tasty, crowd-pleasing recipes that are perfect for taking to fun events anytime of the year. Whether you're searching for a traditional picnic food or something new to share with your friends and family, you'll find it in here! With classics like Picnic Fried Chicken and German Potato Salad, plus new favorites like Fresh Peach Salsa, Teriyaki Steak Kabobs and Key Lime Pretzel Surprise, your menu contribution is sure to satisfy!

Tips for Menu Planning

Before you whip up something fabulous, take a moment to plan the appropriate menu items. The following tips are helpful when planning foods for a crowd.

- Take only the amount of food you think will be eaten.
  It is easier to bring home empty containers than to tote around leftovers.
- Plan for a way to keep cold foods cold and hot foods hot.
- Pack condiments in small containers rather than taking whole jars.
- If a cooler is not available, some food suggestions are:
  Fruit (fresh, canned or dried)
  Raw vegetables
  Hard cheese
  Canned or dried meat or fish
  Bread
  Peanut butter
  Crackers or dry snack mixes
  Chips or cookies

Tips for Packing Containers to Keep Food HOT

Hot Packs

- Conserve heat by wrapping hot dish containers in towels, aluminum foil or newspaper.
- Slow cookers with a ceramic insert are ideal for keeping food hot if an electric source is available. A slow cooker with a ceramic insert that is not plugged into an outlet will keep food warm for a short amount of time.
- Insulated thermoses or dishes are also handy for keeping food warm.
- Fill a thermos-type container with very hot water for 10 to 15 minutes before filling with hot food. Pour out hot water immediately before placing food in the container.

At the Event

- Keep lids, covers and wraps on containers until serving time.
- If an electrical outlet is available, plug in slow cookers or hot plates upon arrival.
- Discard any leftover hot foods that cannot be refrigerated immediately after they are done being served.
- Ideally, hot foods should be kept above 140°F.

Tips for Packing Coolers to Keep Food COLD

Freezer Packs

- There are many types of freezer packs available, everything from commercial gel-filled packs to a homemade ice pack. To make an ice pack at home, fill a leak-proof plastic container with water and place in freezer until frozen. Or, fill a plastic bag with ice cubes and wrap the plastic bag in aluminum foil. Frozen foods in containers, such as juice packs, yogurt or applesauce, also work well as freezer packs.

- Use a cooler that will keep food at 40°F, or plan to take foods that are less perishable.

- A freezer pack can keep cold food cold for up to four hours. Make sure the food is cold BEFORE placing it in the cooler. Cooked foods should be chilled thoroughly before placing in the cooler. Precook any meat until done, and then chill before placing in the cooler.

- Pack the cold foods tightly together and place the freezer packs on TOP of all the food. Close the cooler tightly.

- Pack cold foods and cold drinks in separate coolers, since the drink cooler will be opened more often.

- To transport, place the cooler inside the vehicle rather than in the hot trunk or bed of the truck.

At the Event

- Place the cooler in a cool area, such as under the shade of a tree or under a shelter.

- Keep the lid on the cooler and do not open the cooler more than necessary. Retrieve items quickly and replace the cooler lid.

- If possible, add more ice to the cooler as the original ice melts.

- Do not let cold food sit out of the cooler for a long period of time. Serve cold foods quickly, or serve them in small portions.

- To serve a chilled salad, fill a large bowl with ice. Place the salad in a smaller bowl and set inside the ice-filled bowl.

Tips for Food Safety and Grilling

Handling Food Properly

- Wash hands, utensils, plates and cooking surfaces before and after they come in contact with any food.
- Meats intended for grilling should be kept separate from other food so there is no chance for bacterial contamination.
- Pack separate utensils and cutting boards for use with raw meats and cooked meats. Utensils and cutting boards that have come in contact with raw meat should be washed in hot soapy water after use.
- Once cold foods have been out in the open for more than two hours, toss them out. If the outdoor temperature is 90° or higher, decrease the "safe" time to one hour.

Safe Grilling

- Food that will be grilled should be removed from the cooler just before grilling. Do not remove it all at once if the food will not be grilled right away.
- The USDA recommends fully cooking meats to ensure bacteria is destroyed. Hamburgers and ribs should be cooked to 160°F or until the center is no longer pink and the meat juices run clear. Cook ground poultry to 165°F and poultry parts to 180°F. Use an accurate meat thermometer to monitor the temperatures.
- When meat is fully cooked, transfer it to a clean plate or platter. NEVER place cooked meat on a surface that held raw foods.
- Reheat meats that have been pre-cooked until they are steaming hot.
- Never reuse marinades that have come in contact with raw meat, chicken or fish. Discard all marinades after use, even those used just for brushing or basting.

Finger
Foods

Classic Deviled Eggs

Makes 12 servings

Ingredients

6 eggs

½ tsp. paprika

2 T. mayonnaise

½ tsp. dry mustard

Fresh parsley sprigs, optional

Directions

Place eggs in a medium pot of lightly salted water. Bring the water to a boil and after 1 minute, reduce heat to low and cook eggs for approximately 10 more minutes. Drain eggs and cool. (Speed method is to immerse the cooked eggs in ice water for 5 to 10 minutes.) Peel eggs and cut each egg in half lengthwise. Transfer egg yolks into a small bowl and mash with a fork. Mix in the paprika, mayonnaise and dry mustard. Spoon the yolk mixture into the egg halves; cool and serve. Eggs may be garnished with sprigs of fresh parsley, if desired.

Spicy Deviled Eggs

Makes 12 servings

Ingredients

6 eggs

1 T. spicy brown mustard

1 T. Italian salad dressing

¼ C. mayonnaise

½ tsp. pepper

½ tsp. salt

Pinch of paprika

Directions

Place eggs in a medium pot of lightly salted water. Bring the water to a boil and after 1 minute, reduce heat to low and cook eggs for approximately 10 more minutes. Drain eggs and cool. (Speed method is to immerse the cooked eggs in ice water for 5 to 10 minutes.) Peel eggs and cut each egg in half lengthwise. Transfer egg yolks into a small bowl and mash with a fork. Mix in the mustard, Italian dressing, mayonnaise and pepper. Arrange the egg white halves on a plate and sprinkle with salt. Spoon the yolk mixture into the egg halves and sprinkle with paprika. Refrigerate until ready to serve.

Sun-Dried Tomato Dip

Makes 1 cups

Ingredients

¼ C. oil-packed sun-dried tomatoes, drained and chopped

1 (8 oz.) pkg. cream cheese, softened

½ C. sour cream

¼ C. mayonnaise

2 cloves garlic, peeled

Hot pepper sauce to taste

¾ tsp. salt

¾ tsp. freshly ground pepper

2 to 4 T. fresh basil, as desired

Directions

In a food processor, place the chopped sun-dried tomatoes, cream cheese, sour cream, mayonnaise, garlic cloves, hot pepper sauce, salt and pepper. Process until well blended. Add basil and continue processing until smooth. Transfer to a serving bowl or dish and refrigerate at least 1 hour before serving. Serve with fresh vegetables or crackers for dipping.

Baked Feta Cheese Dip

Makes 2 cups

Ingredients

1 (16 oz.) pkg. feta cheese, crumbled

12 to 15 cherry tomatoes, finely chopped

1 T. olive oil

2 tsp. minced garlic

Onion powder

Directions

Preheat oven to 400°. In a small baking dish, combine feta cheese, finely chopped tomatoes, olive oil and minced garlic. Season with onion powder to taste. Bake for 15 to 20 minutes or until olive oil is bubbling. Serve in baking dish with bread for dipping.

Spinach & Artichoke Dip in a Bread Bowl

Makes 4 to 5 cups

Ingredients

1 (16 oz.) carton sour cream

1 (1 oz.) pkg. dry ranch dressing mix

1 (14 oz.) can artichoke hearts, drained, rinsed and chopped

1 (10 oz.) pkg. frozen chopped spinach, thawed and well drained

1 (2 oz.) jar diced pimentos, drained and rinsed

1 (1½ lb.) round loaf bread, any kind

Directions

In a medium bowl, combine sour cream and ranch dressing mix. Stir in chopped artichokes, spinach and pimentos; set aside. Prepare bread bowl by slicing off top 1″ of round loaf of bread. Hollow out center of bread, leaving a 1″ shell. Tear the removed bread into pieces and reserve for dipping. Spoon dip into bread shell. May be served warm or cold. To serve warm, place filled bread bowl on a baking sheet and bake in 400° oven for 20 to 25 minutes. Cover loaf with aluminum foil if the bread browns too quickly. Serve with bread cubes or assorted fresh vegetables for dipping.

Layered Barbecue Bean Dip

Makes 10 to 12 servings

Ingredients

1 (16 oz.) can barbecue-style baked beans

1 C. chopped tomatoes

2 C. shredded lettuce

1 C. shredded sharp Cheddar cheese

½ C. sour cream

½ C. peppercorn ranch salad dressing

5 slices bacon, cooked and crumbled

¼ C. sliced green onions

Directions

In a 9″ pie plate or serving dish, create layers of baked beans, chopped tomatoes, shredded lettuce and shredded cheese. In a small bowl, combine sour cream and ranch dressing. Spoon sour cream mixture over shredded cheese layer. Sprinkle with crumbled bacon and green onions. Serve immediately or cover and refrigerate up to 2 hours. Serve with tortilla chips for dipping.

Deluxe Olive Spread

Makes 24 servings

Ingredients

1 C. pitted black olives

1 C. pitted green olives

1 C. pitted kalamata olives

2 cloves garlic, peeled

3 T. balsamic vinegar

3 T. olive oil

Directions

In a food processor, place the black olives, green olives, kalamata olives and garlic cloves; pulse to chop. Then add balsamic vinegar and olive oil. Process until smooth. Refrigerate at least 1 hour, or overnight if possible. Serve as a spread for crackers or thin bread slices.

Shrimp Dip Supreme

Makes 2 cups

Ingredients

2 (4½ oz.) cans salad shrimp, drained

1 T. lemon juice

¼ C. finely chopped onion

1 (3 oz.) pkg. cream cheese, softened

Mayonnaise, approximately 2 T.

Directions

In a medium bowl, combine shrimp, lemon juice, chopped onion, cream cheese and enough mayonnaise to make mixture a good dipping consistency. Transfer to a serving bowl or dish and refrigerate until ready to serve. Serve with raw vegetables or crackers for dipping.

Fresh Peach Salsa

Makes 3 cups

Ingredients

6 large fresh peaches, peeled, pitted and chopped

⅔ C. orange marmalade

¼ C. sliced green onions

3 T. cider vinegar

1 oz. crystallized ginger

2 tsp. sugar

Directions

In a medium bowl, combine chopped peaches, orange marmalade, green onions, cider vinegar, crystallized ginger and sugar. Toss together until well combined. Cover and refrigerate until ready to serve with chips and crackers for dipping.

Party Favorite Cheese Ball

Makes 3 cups

Ingredients

2 (8 oz.) pkgs. cream cheese, softened

1 C. shredded dried beef

⅓ C. zesty Italian salad dressing

¾ C. chopped pecans

Directions

In a medium bowl, combine cream cheese, shredded dried beef and Italian dressing. Mix thoroughly with a fork until well blended. Chill in refrigerator for 1 hour and then shape into a ball. Roll cheese ball in chopped pecans and serve with crackers for dipping.

Picnic Pita Wedges

Makes 16 pieces

Ingredients

3 T. olive oil

¼ tsp. dried oregano

¼ tsp. sea salt

¼ tsp. pepper

1 T. butter

2 (6") pita pockets

16 slices pepperoni

4 round slices provolone cheese

½ C. medium chunky salsa

Directions

Preheat oven to 375°. In a microwave-safe bowl, combine olive oil, oregano, sea salt and pepper. Heat for approximately 30 seconds. Remove from microwave and add butter; stir and set aside. Cut each pita pocket into 8 pieces using the following method: Cut each pita pocket in half, then cut each in half again to make 4 wedges. Cut along curved outer edge to separate each wedge into 2 pieces. Brush both sides of the pita wedges with warm olive oil mixture, coating well. On a large baking sheet, place wedges, crust side down. Spread 1 teaspoon salsa on top of each wedge. Cut provolone slices into 4 wedge-shaped pieces and place one on top of each pita wedge. Top each with 1 slice of pepperoni and drizzle with any remaining olive oil mixture. Sprinkle pita wedges with additional coarse sea salt and bake for 15 minutes or until golden brown. Serve warm.

Mozzarella Cheese Sticks

Makes 18 pieces

Ingredients

2 eggs

1 C. fine cracker crumbs

9 pieces mozzarella string
cheese, cut in half

3 T. olive oil

Directions

In a medium bowl, lightly beat eggs. Place the cracker crumbs in a shallow dish. Dip the string cheese pieces into the egg and then into the crumbs. In a medium skillet over medium-high heat, fry mozzarella sticks in oil until coating is crisp and golden brown. Drain on paper towels, then arrange mozzarella sticks on a serving plate. Serve with marinara sauce for dipping.

Tomato Basil Squares

Makes 36 squares

Ingredients

1 (12 oz.) pkg. refrigerated
pizza crust dough

2 C. shredded mozzarella
cheese, divided

¼ C. grated Parmesan cheese

2 T. fresh chopped basil
or 2 tsp. dried basil

⅔ C. mayonnaise

1 clove garlic

4 plum tomatoes, thinly sliced

Directions

Preheat oven to 375°. Roll pizza dough out onto a lightly greased 12 x 15" baking sheet, leaving 1" around edges. Sprinkle crust with 1 cup mozzarella cheese; set aside. In a medium bowl, combine remaining 1 cup mozzarella cheese, Parmesan cheese, basil and mayonnaise. Use a garlic press to press garlic clove. Add crushed garlic clove to mayonnaise mixture and blend thoroughly; set aside. Arrange tomato slices over mozzarella cheese on pizza dough. Spread the mayonnaise mixture over the tomatoes. Bake for 15 to 20 minutes or until topping is golden brown and bubbly. Cut into about 36 squares and serve warm.

Artichoke Balls

Makes approximately 24 balls

Ingredients

1 (6 oz.) jar marinated artichoke hearts

2 eggs

1 T. garlic juice

1 T. Worcestershire sauce

½ tsp. liquid smoke

½ tsp. hot pepper sauce

1 (14 oz.) can artichoke hearts, packed in water

1½ C. Italian seasoned breadcrumbs

⅓ C. fresh grated Parmesan cheese

Directions

Drain and finely chop the 6 ounce jar of marinated artichoke hearts, reserving the liquid marinade. In a medium bowl, beat eggs with reserved marinade. Add garlic juice, Worcestershire sauce, liquid smoke and hot pepper sauce; mix well. Drain and finely chop the 14 ounce can of water-packed artichokes. Mix all of the chopped artichokes and breadcrumbs into the artichoke marinade mixture, blending thoroughly. Form mixture into small balls and roll each ball in grated Parmesan cheese. Refrigerate for at least 1 hour to allow flavors to blend. Preheat oven to 300°. On a lightly greased baking sheet, place artichoke balls and bake for 7 to 10 minutes. Serve immediately.

Tarragon Mushroom Triangles

Makes 24 pieces

Ingredients

1 T. olive oil

½ C. chopped red onions

2 tsp. dried tarragon

⅛ tsp. cayenne pepper

1 C. coarsely chopped fresh mushrooms

½ C. frozen chopped spinach, thawed and drained

¼ C. chopped roasted sweet red peppers

2 oz. feta cheese, crumbled

Pinch of grated nutmeg

16 sheets of phyllo dough, thawed

4 T. butter, melted

Directions

Preheat oven to 350°. In a large frying pan over medium heat, warm the oil. Add the chopped red onions, tarragon and cayenne pepper; sauté for 4 minutes, stirring frequently. Add the chopped mushrooms and cook for an additional 6 to 8 minutes, or until all the liquid has evaporated. Transfer this mixture to a large bowl; add the spinach and red peppers. Mix in the feta cheese and nutmeg, stirring well.

Unroll the phyllo dough and cover it with a piece of plastic to keep it from drying out. Peel off 2 sheets and lay the double layer on a flat work surface. Cut the phyllo into thirds lengthwise; brush lightly with butter. Place 1 tablespoon of filling in the bottom corner of each strip. Fold over once to make a triangle; continue folding over as if folding a flag; place on baking sheet. Repeat, using all the remaining phyllo and spinach mixture. Brush tops of triangles with remaining butter. Bake for 12 to 15 minutes, or until triangles are golden. Serve warm.

Cheese Crunchies

Makes 15 servings

Ingredients

2½ C. Corn Chex cereal, crushed

¾ tsp. chili seasoning powder

½ C. plus 2 T. butter, divided

1¼ C. shredded sharp Cheddar cheese

1 C. flour

½ tsp. onion powder

¼ tsp. seasoned salt

Directions

Preheat oven to 350°. In a small bowl, combine crushed Chex cereal and chili seasoning. Melt 2 tablespoons butter in microwave or over stovetop; set aside. In a medium bowl, blend shredded Cheddar cheese and remaining ½ cup softened butter. Blend in flour, ½ cup of the seasoned Chex mixture, onion powder and seasoned salt. Shape into 1″ balls and roll in remaining crumbs. Place on baking sheet. With the bottom of a glass, flatten each ball to ¼″ thickness. Bake for 12 to 14 minutes or until deep golden in color. Serve warm.

Spicy Pretzels

Makes 20 servings

Ingredients

1 C. vegetable oil

1 (1 oz.) pkg. dry ranch
    dressing mix

1 tsp. garlic salt

1 tsp. cayenne pepper

1 (20 oz.) bag round
    mini pretzels

Directions

Preheat oven to 200°. In a small bowl, combine vegetable oil, ranch dressing mix, garlic salt and cayenne pepper; blend well. Place pretzels in an even layer in a large roasting pan. Pour seasoned liquid mixture over pretzels and stir to coat completely. Bake, uncovered, for 2 hours, stirring after every 20 minutes. Spread coated pretzels on paper towels to cool. Store in an air-tight container.

Classic Chex Party Mix

Makes 15 servings

Ingredients

6 T. butter

1 tsp. seasoned salt

4 tsp. Worcestershire sauce

2 C. Corn Chex cereal

2 C. Rice Chex cereal

2 C. Wheat Chex cereal

1½ C. mixed nuts

Directions

Preheat oven to 250°. In a large Dutch oven or shallow roasting pan over low heat, melt butter. Stir in seasoned salt and Worcestershire sauce. Add cereals and nuts, stirring until all pieces are coated. Heat in oven for 45 minutes, stirring after every 15 minutes. Spread party mix on paper towels to cool. Store in an air-tight container.

Hot & Spicy Party Mix

Makes 15 servings

Ingredients

½ C. butter

1½ tsp. salt

1 tsp. onion powder

½ tsp. chili powder

4½ tsp. Worcestershire sauce

½ tsp. hot pepper sauce

2 C. Rice Chex cereal

2 C. Bran Chex cereal

2 C. Wheat Chex cereal

1 C. salted nuts

Directions

Preheat oven to 250°. In a large Dutch oven or shallow roasting pan, place butter. Place pan in oven and melt butter. Remove from oven and stir in salt, onion powder, chili powder, Worcestershire sauce and hot pepper sauce. Add cereals and nuts. Mix well, stirring until all pieces are coated. Heat in oven for 1 hour, stirring after every 15 minutes. Spread party mix on paper towels to cool. Store in an air-tight container.

Caramel Snack Mix

Makes 20 servings

Ingredients

½ C. butter

¾ C. light corn syrup

1 C. brown sugar

1 (12 oz.) pkg. Corn Chex cereal

1 C. chopped pecans

1 C. almonds

Directions

Preheat oven to 275°. Spray a large Dutch oven or shallow roasting pan with non-stick cooking spray. In a medium microwave-safe bowl, mix butter, corn syrup and brown sugar. Place mixture in the microwave and cook for 2 minutes, or until butter melts. Place cereal, pecans and almonds in the prepared roasting pan. Pour melted butter mixture over the cereal and nuts; mix gently until cereal and nuts are coated. Bake for 1 hour, stirring after every 15 minutes. Remove caramel mixture from oven. It is important to continue stirring while mixture is cooling to keep it from sticking together. Store in an airtight container.

Brie with Pesto & Sun-Dried Tomatoes

Makes 6 servings

Ingredients

1 (8 oz.) round brie cheese

2 T. pesto

6 oil-packed sun-dried tomatoes, drained and chopped

Directions

Preheat oven to 350°. Place round of brie cheese on an oven-proof dish and top with pesto and chopped sun-dried tomatoes. Bake for 15 to 20 minutes. Serve warm with crackers or fresh crisp Italian bread for dipping.

Olive Cheese Puffs

Makes 50 pieces

Ingredients

2 C. shredded sharp Cheddar cheese

½ C. butter, softened

1 tsp. paprika

1 C. flour

50 green olives, drained well

Directions

Preheat oven to 400°. In a medium bowl, blend the shredded Cheddar cheese, butter, paprika and flour; mix well. Wrap 1 teaspoon of dough around each olive, covering it completely. Place balls on a baking sheet and bake for 15 minutes. Serve warm.

Salads

Classic Macaroni Salad

Makes 10 servings

Ingredients

4 C. elbow macaroni, uncooked

1 C. mayonnaise

¼ C. vinegar

⅔ C. sugar

2½ T. yellow mustard

1½ tsp. salt

½ tsp. pepper

1 large onion, chopped

2 stalks celery, chopped

1 green bell pepper, chopped

¼ C. grated carrot, optional

2 T. chopped pimento peppers, optional

Directions

Bring a large pot of lightly salted water to a boil. Add the macaroni and cook until tender, about 8 minutes. Rinse under cold water and drain. In a large bowl, mix together the mayonnaise, vinegar, sugar, mustard, salt and pepper. Stir in the chopped onion, chopped celery, chopped green pepper, grated carrot, chopped pimentos and cooked macaroni. Cover and refrigerate at least 4 hours before serving.

Broccoli & Tortellini Salad

Makes 12 servings

Ingredients

6 slices bacon

1 (20 oz.) pkg. fresh or frozen cheese-filled tortellini

½ C. mayonnaise

½ C. sugar

2 tsp. cider vinegar

3 heads fresh broccoli, cut into florets

1 C. raisins

1 C. sunflower seeds

1 red onion, finely chopped

Directions

In a large skillet over medium-high heat, brown bacon; drain, crumble and set aside. Bring a large pot of lightly salted water to a boil. Cook tortellini in boiling water for 8 to 10 minutes or until cooked but still firm. Drain and rinse tortellini under cold water. In a small bowl, mix together mayonnaise, sugar and vinegar to make the dressing. In a large bowl, combine cooked tortellini, crumbled bacon, broccoli florets, raisins, sunflower seeds and chopped red onion. Pour dressing over salad and toss. Cover and refrigerate at least 1 hour before serving.

Feta & Tomato Pasta Salad

Makes 8 servings

Ingredients

1 (16 oz.) pkg. spiral pasta

2 green onions, chopped

1 (6 oz.) pkg. feta cheese, crumbled

½ C. balsamic vinegar

¼ C. extra virgin olive oil

2 C. chopped fresh tomato

Directions

Bring a large pot of lightly salted water to a boil. Cook pasta in boiling water for 8 to 10 minutes or until cooked but still firm. Drain and rinse pasta under cold water. In a large bowl, toss pasta with chopped green onions, feta cheese, balsamic vinegar, olive oil and chopped tomato. Cover and refrigerate at least 1 hour before serving.

Antipasto Pasta Salad

Makes 12 servings

Ingredients

1 lb. small seashell pasta

¼ lb. Genoa salami, chopped

¼ lb. pepperoni sausage, chopped

½ lb. Asiago cheese, diced

1 (6 oz.) can sliced black olives, drained

1 red bell pepper, chopped

1 green bell pepper, chopped

3 tomatoes, chopped

1 (1 oz.) env. dry Italian-style salad dressing mix

¾ C. extra virgin olive oil

¼ C. balsamic vinegar

2 T. dried oregano

1 T. dried parsley

1 T. grated Parmesan cheese

Salt

Pepper

Directions

Bring a large pot of lightly salted water to a boil. Cook pasta in boiling water for 8 to 10 minutes or until cooked but still firm. Drain and rinse pasta under cold water. In a large bowl, combine the cooked pasta, chopped salami, chopped pepperoni, diced Asiago cheese and sliced black olives. Add the chopped red bell pepper, green bell pepper and tomatoes. Stir in the envelope of dry salad dressing mix. Cover and refrigerate at least 1 hour. To prepare the liquid dressing, whisk together the olive oil, balsamic vinegar, oregano, parsley, Parmesan cheese, salt and pepper. Just before serving, pour dressing over the salad and mix well.

Great American Potato Salad

Makes 6 servings

Ingredients

1 C. mayonnaise or
  salad dressing

1 tsp. yellow mustard

½ tsp. celery seed

½ tsp. salt

⅛ tsp. pepper

4 C. cooked and cubed
  potatoes

2 hard-cooked eggs,
  peeled and chopped

½ C. chopped onion

½ C. sliced celery

½ C. sweet pickle relish

Directions

In a large bowl, combine salad dressing, mustard, celery seed, salt and pepper; mix well. Stir in the cooked potatoes, chopped eggs, chopped onion, sliced celery and pickle relish; mix lightly. Cover and refrigerate until ready to serve.

Tangy Dijon Potato Salad

Makes 12 to 14 servings

Ingredients

5 lbs. potatoes, peeled and cubed

2 to 3 stalks celery, finely chopped

1 medium onion, finely chopped

¼ C. stemmed and chopped fresh cilantro

6 hard-cooked eggs, peeled and chopped

¼ C. cider vinegar

1 T. Dijon mustard

1 C. mayonnaise or salad dressing

Salt

Pepper

3 ripe tomatoes, cut into wedges

1 cucumber, sliced

Directions

Bring a large pot of lightly salted water to a boil. Cook potatoes in boiling water for 8 to 10 minutes or until cooked but still firm; drain. Place drained potatoes in large bowl of ice water to cool quickly; drain again after potatoes are cool. In a large bowl, mix potatoes, chopped celery, chopped onion, cilantro and chopped eggs; set aside. In a small bowl, whisk together vinegar, mustard, salad dressing, salt and pepper to taste; fold mayonnaise mixture into potato mixture. Cover and refrigerate for at least 1 hour. Garnish with tomato wedges and cucumber slices before serving.

Zesty Potato Salad

Makes 8 servings

Ingredients

4 C. cooked and cubed potatoes

½ C. chopped celery

2 hard-cooked eggs, peeled and chopped

¼ C. sliced green onions

1 tsp. salt

⅛ tsp. pepper

1 C. mayonnaise or salad dressing

1 tsp. yellow mustard

¼ tsp. celery seed

1 tsp. horseradish

Dash of hot pepper sauce, optional

1 T. cider vinegar

Directions

In a large bowl, toss together cooked potatoes, chopped celery, eggs, green onions, salt and pepper. In a small bowl, mix salad dressing, mustard, celery seed, horseradish, hot pepper sauce and vinegar. Stir salad dressing mixture into potato mixture. Cover and refrigerate for at least 1 hour before serving.

German Potato Salad

Makes 12 servings

Ingredients

1 lb. bacon

9 medium potatoes, peeled, sliced and cooked

1 large onion, sliced thin

½ C. flour

1¼ C. vinegar

½ C. sugar

Directions

In a large skillet over medium-high heat, cook bacon until crisp; drain and crumble, reserving bacon grease in skillet. In a large bowl, toss together crumbled bacon, cooked potatoes and sliced onion; set aside. In the skillet with remaining bacon grease, mix in flour, then whisk in vinegar and 2¼ cups water. Add sugar and continue cooking, stirring constantly until thickened. Pour over potato mixture and serve warm.

Mandarin-Walnut Mixed Green Salad

Makes 6 to 8 servings

Ingredients

6 C. torn mixed salad greens

1½ C. mandarin oranges, drained

1¼ C. chopped walnuts

½ C. orange juice

2 T. balsamic vinegar

1 T. olive oil

1 T. honey

1 T. Dijon mustard

1 T. soy sauce

1½ tsp. minced gingerroot

3 cloves garlic, minced

Directions

In a large bowl, place salad greens, oranges and chopped walnuts; toss lightly. In a blender or food processor, combine the orange juice, balsamic vinegar, olive oil, honey, mustard, soy sauce, minced gingerroot and minced garlic; blend thoroughly and set aside. Drizzle dressing over salad greens just before serving.

Nutty Garden Salad

Makes 8 servings

Ingredients

½ C. olive oil

¼ C. cider vinegar

2 T. plus 2 tsp. sugar

1 tsp. salt

½ tsp. pepper

8 C. torn salad greens

1½ C. sliced zucchini

4 medium carrots, sliced

4 stalks celery, sliced

4 green onions, sliced

½ C. seasoned croutons

2 T. whole almonds, toasted*

2 T. sesame seeds, toasted**

Directions

In a jar or bowl with a tight-fitting lid, combine olive oil, vinegar, sugar, salt and pepper; replace lid and shake well. In a large bowl, toss together salad greens, sliced zucchini, sliced carrots, sliced celery and sliced green onions. Dress greens and vegetables with oil mixture just before serving. Top with croutons, toasted almonds and toasted sesame seeds.

*To toast almonds: Preheat oven to 350°. Place almonds on a baking sheet and toast for 10 to 15 minutes or until they have cracked and smell like popcorn. The almonds may also be toasted under the oven broiler for 5 to 10 minutes.

**To toast sesame seeds: Heat seeds in a wide frying pan over medium heat on the stovetop, shaking the pan occasionally. Remove the seeds when they darken and become fragrant.

Pepper Parmesan Mixed Green Salad

Makes 8 servings

Ingredients

⅓ C. chopped carrots

⅓ C. chopped celery

2 T. chopped onion

6 T. sugar

6 T. vegetable oil

¼ C. cider vinegar

¼ tsp. salt

8 C. torn salad greens

1 medium yellow bell pepper, chopped

1 medium green bell pepper, chopped

¾ C. shredded Parmesan cheese

¾ C. halved cherry tomatoes

Directions

In a blender or food processor, combine chopped carrots, chopped celery, chopped onion, sugar, oil, vinegar and salt; process until smooth. In a large bowl, mix the salad greens, chopped yellow pepper, chopped green pepper, Parmesan cheese and cherry tomato halves. Drizzle with dressing just before serving; toss to coat.

Italian Garden Salad

Makes 6 to 8 servings

Ingredients

2 red bell peppers, diced

2 green bell peppers, diced

2 tomatoes, chopped

4 stalks celery, chopped

1 C. bean sprouts

½ onion, diced, optional

½ C. Italian salad dressing, or to taste

Directions

In a large bowl, toss together diced red bell pepper, diced green bell pepper, chopped tomatoes, chopped celery, bean sprouts and diced onion. Stir in the Italian dressing just before serving.

Balsamic Green Bean Salad

Makes 4 servings

Ingredients

1 lb. fresh green beans, trimmed

2 T. chopped green onions

2 T. minced garlic

¼ C. balsamic vinegar

¼ C. olive oil

Directions

Bring a large pot of lightly salted water to a boil. Cook green beans in boiling water for 8 to 10 minutes or until cooked but still firm; drain and cool. In a medium bowl, stir together green onions, garlic, balsamic vinegar and oil; pour over green beans. Cover and refrigerate for at least 1 hour before serving.

Avocado Tomato Salad

Makes 4 servings

Ingredients

1 large or 2 medium avocados, peeled and pitted

2 tsp. lemon juice

1 pint cherry tomatoes

¼ medium-sized sweet onion, sliced thin

3 T. rice vinegar

Salt

Coarsely ground black pepper

1 T. olive oil

Directions

Cut avocado into 1″ chunks and sprinkle with lemon juice. Wash cherry tomatoes and cut each one in half. In a medium bowl, mix together avocado chunks, tomato halves and onion slices. Sprinkle rice vinegar over the avocado mixture and mix gently. Add salt and pepper to taste. Just before serving, drizzle olive oil over mixture and gently stir until all ingredients are well combined.

Picnic Coleslaw

Makes 8 servings

Ingredients

1½ C. sugar

¾ C. vegetable oil

¾ C. vinegar

1 tsp. salt

1 large head cabbage, shredded

2 carrots, shredded

1 green bell pepper, finely chopped

1 medium onion, finely chopped

Directions

In a medium saucepan over medium-high heat, combine sugar, oil, vinegar and salt. Bring to a boil for 1 to 2 minutes, stirring constantly; set aside. In a large bowl, combine shredded cabbage, shredded carrots, chopped green pepper and chopped onion. Pour warm vinegar mixture over vegetable mixture. Cover and refrigerate for several hours before serving.

Crunchy Cabbage Salad

Makes 6 to 8 servings

Ingredients

½ large head cabbage, shredded

½ bunch broccoli, chopped

½ head cauliflower, broken into florets

4 green onions, chopped

1 (3 oz.) pkg. chicken-flavored ramen noodles, toasted*

½ C. slivered almonds, toasted*

2 T. sesame seeds, toasted*

½ C. vegetable oil

3 T. cider vinegar

2 T. sugar

1 tsp. salt

Directions

Remove seasoning packet from ramen noodles and set aside. In a large bowl, combine shredded cabbage, chopped broccoli, cauliflower florets and green onions. Mix in the toasted ramen noodles, toasted almonds and toasted sesame seeds. In a small bowl, whisk together vegetable oil, cider vinegar, sugar and salt until well blended. Mix in seasoning packet from ramen noodles and pour dressing over cabbage mixture; toss well to coat. Cover and refrigerate for at least 1 hour before serving.

*To toast ramen noodles, almonds and sesame seeds: Preheat oven to 350°. Place broken ramen noodles, slivered almonds and sesame seeds in an even layer on a baking sheet. Place baking sheet in preheated oven for 10 to 15 minutes or until noodles, almonds and sesame seeds are golden brown.

Easy Pickled Beets

Makes 18 servings

Ingredients

1 T. mixed pickling spice

2 C. vinegar

2 C. sugar

1 tsp. cinnamon

1 tsp. salt

4 (16 oz.) cans sliced beets

Directions

Place pickling spices in a cheesecloth bag. In a large saucepan over medium-high heat, combine vinegar, sugar, cinnamon, salt and the spice bag; bring to a boil. Drain the beets, reserving ¾ cup of juice. Add beets and reserved juice to the large saucepan; stir well. Pour beets and liquid into a 1½–quart glass container. Cover and refrigerate overnight. Remove spice bag before serving.

Minty Melon Medley

Makes 4 to 6 servings

Ingredients

1½ C. cubed honeydew melon

1½ C. cubed cantaloupe

¼ C. dry sherry wine

2 T. chopped fresh mint leaves

1 sprig mint leaves for garnish

Directions

In a medium bowl, gently toss the honeydew and cantaloupe melon cubes with sherry wine and chopped mint leaves. Cover and refrigerate for 1 hour to blend flavors. Serve from the bowl or spoon into individual bowls and garnish with a mint leaf.

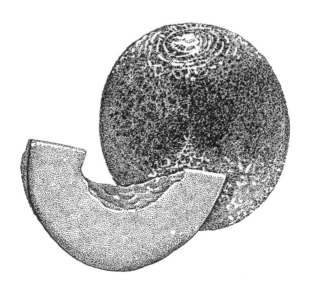

Fresh Strawberry Salad

Makes 12 servings

Ingredients

1 (3 oz.) pkg. ramen noodles, any flavor

¼ C. butter

1 C. chopped walnuts

¼ C. vegetable oil

¼ C. sugar

2 T. red wine vinegar

½ tsp. soy sauce

8 C. torn romaine lettuce

½ C. chopped green onions

2 C. sliced fresh strawberries

Directions

Remove seasoning packet from ramen noodles and set aside for another use. Break ramen noodles into small pieces. In a small skillet over medium heat, melt butter. Add broken noodles and chopped walnuts; sauté until golden. Cool and set aside. In a jar with a tight-fitting lid, combine oil, sugar, vinegar and soy sauce. Replace lid and shake until well blended. In a large bowl, combine the romaine lettuce, chopped green onions, sliced strawberries and cooled noodle mixture. Drizzle with dressing just before serving; toss gently.

Sunflower Fruit Salad

Makes 4 servings

Ingredients

2 medium apples, chopped

1 medium firm banana, sliced

⅓ C. sunflower seeds

¼ C. halved green grapes

¼ C. chopped celery

¼ C. plain yogurt

Directions

In a medium bowl, combine the chopped apples, banana slices, sunflower seeds, grape halves and chopped celery. Add plain yogurt and stir gently to coat. Cover and refrigerate until ready to serve.

Honey Apple Salad

Makes 6 servings

Ingredients

1 medium Golden Delicious apple, chopped

1 medium red apple, chopped

2 stalks celery, thinly sliced

½ C. chopped walnuts

½ C. golden raisins

¼ C. honey

Directions

In a medium bowl, combine the chopped apple, sliced celery, chopped walnuts and golden raisins. Add the honey right before serving and mix well. Serve immediately.

Casseroles
& Deep
Dishes

Wonderfully Easy Lasagna

Makes 8 servings

Ingredients

1 (8 oz.) pkg. lasagna noodles

1 lb. lean ground beef

½ C. chopped onion

1 (8 oz.) can sliced mushrooms, drained, optional

1 (16 oz.) jar spaghetti sauce, any kind

1 tsp. garlic powder

½ tsp. salt

1 tsp. dried oregano

½ tsp. dried basil

1½ C. ricotta cheese

1 (16 oz.) pkg. shredded Monterey Jack cheese

¾ C. grated Parmesan cheese

Directions

Preheat oven to 350°. Cook lasagna noodles according to package directions; drain and set aside. In a large skillet over medium heat, combine ground beef, chopped onion and sliced mushrooms. Cook until meat is no longer pink; drain well. Add spaghetti sauce, garlic powder, salt, oregano and basil; simmer for 30 minutes. Grease the bottom and sides of a 7 x 11" baking dish. Place ⅓ of the cooked lasagna noodles on the bottom of the baking dish. Spread ⅓ of the ricotta cheese on top of noodles, then ⅓ of the meat sauce, followed by ⅓ of the Monterey Jack cheese and end with ⅓ of the Parmesan cheese. Repeat layers two more times. Bake for 30 minutes or until hot and bubbly. Let stand for 8 to 10 minutes before cutting.

Italian Ziti Casserole

Makes 8 servings

Ingredients

1 (16 oz.) pkg. ziti pasta

1 lb. ground Italian sausage

2 carrots, peeled

2 stalks celery

1 medium onion, chopped

1½ C. milk

2 T. flour

1 (28 oz.) can crushed tomatoes

1 tsp. sugar

½ tsp. dried basil

¼ tsp. pepper

1 (16 oz.) pkg. shredded mozzarella cheese, divided

Directions

Preheat oven to 375°. In a large saucepan, cook ziti pasta according to package directions using the minimum cooking time required; drain immediately and return pasta to pan. In a large skillet over medium-high heat, cook sausage until browned. While browning, break up sausage with a wooden spoon. Once cooked through, remove sausage with a slotted spoon, reserving drippings in skillet. Cut carrots and celery into ½" slices. Place skillet with sausage drippings over medium-high heat. Add carrots, celery and chopped onion. Sauté until vegetables are almost tender, stirring occasionally. In a small bowl, use a fork to mix milk and flour until smooth. Pour mixture over vegetables in skillet and cook until thickened. Add crushed tomatoes in liquid, sugar, basil and pepper; stir and heat to boiling. Carefully pour vegetables into pot with ziti pasta. Add half of the mozzarella cheese and mix well. Grease a 3-quart baking dish. Spoon ziti mixture into baking dish; sprinkle remaining mozzarella cheese over top. Bake for 15 to 20 minutes or until cheese melts and mixture is hot and bubbly.

Turkey Tetrazzini

Makes 6 to 8 servings

Ingredients

1 (4 oz.) pkg. thin spaghetti

3 C. cooked diced turkey

½ C. slivered almonds, toasted*

1 (10¾ oz.) can cream of mushroom soup

1 tsp. Worcestershire sauce

⅛ tsp. nutmeg

½ C. mayonnaise

¼ C. sherry wine

¼ C. heavy whipping cream, whipped

¼ C. grated Parmesan cheese

Directions

Preheat oven to 350°. Cook spaghetti according to package directions; drain. Grease bottom and sides of a 2-quart baking dish. Add cooked spaghetti and layer diced turkey on top. Sprinkle with toasted almonds. In a medium bowl, combine cream of mushroom soup, Worcestershire sauce, nutmeg, mayonnaise, sherry wine and whipped cream; stir well. Pour mixture over ingredients in baking dish. Bake for 30 minutes or until casserole is hot and bubbly.

*To toast almonds: Preheat oven to 350°. Spread slivered almonds in a single layer on a baking sheet. Place in preheated oven and bake for 10 to 15 minutes, stirring occasionally.

Terrific Turkey Swiss Casserole

Makes 4 to 6 servings

Ingredients

1 (10 oz.) pkg. frozen green beans

1 C. cooked chopped turkey

½ C. shredded Swiss cheese

1 (10¾ oz.) can cream of chicken soup

⅛ tsp. nutmeg

1 C. biscuit baking mix

1 egg, beaten

¼ C. butter or margarine, melted

2 T. milk

1 T. fresh chopped parsley

Directions

Preheat oven to 350°. Grease a 2-quart baking dish; set aside. Cook green beans according to package directions without seasoning; drain. Add chopped turkey, shredded Swiss cheese, cream of chicken soup and nutmeg; stir well. Spoon mixture into prepared baking dish. In a small bowl, combine egg, melted butter and milk; stir. In a medium bowl, place biscuit baking mix; use a spoon to form a well in the center. Pour egg mixture into biscuit mix; stir until just blended. Spoon biscuit dough around the edges of green bean mixture leaving center exposed. Sprinkle parsley in center of casserole. Bake for 25 to 30 minutes or until hot and bubbly.

Mediterranean Turkey Medley

Makes 8 servings

Ingredients

1 (16 oz.) pkg. medium egg noodles, uncooked

1 (14½ oz.) can chicken broth

1 C. milk

1 tsp. salt

¼ C. cornstarch

2 C. cooked chopped turkey

1 (14 oz.) can artichoke hearts, drained and quartered

1 (17½ oz.) jar roasted red peppers, drained and sliced

9 ripe olives, pitted and sliced

½ C. shredded mozzarella cheese

½ C. white wine

1 tsp. lemon juice

½ tsp. pepper

3 T. grated Parmesan cheese

Directions

Preheat oven to 350°. Cook noodles according to package directions; drain. In a large saucepan over medium heat, combine chicken broth, milk, salt and cornstarch; stir until cornstarch is dissolved. Cook and stir continually until liquid is thickened and bubbly. Stir in cooked noodles, chopped turkey, quartered artichoke hearts, sliced red peppers, sliced olives, mozzarella cheese, white wine, lemon juice and pepper. Spray a 3-quart baking dish with non-stick vegetable spray. Spoon noodle mixture into baking dish and sprinkle with Parmesan cheese. Bake for 30 to 35 minutes or until bubbly around the edges. Let stand for 5 minutes before serving.

Nutty Chicken Casserole

Makes 8 to 10 servings

Ingredients

4 C. cooked diced chicken

2 C. finely chopped celery

¼ C. finely chopped onion

2 hard-cooked eggs, peeled and chopped

½ C. slivered almonds, toasted*

2 (10¾ oz.) cans cream of chicken soup

¾ C. mayonnaise

½ C. chicken broth

¼ C. lemon juice

½ tsp. salt

¼ tsp. pepper

1 C. crushed round buttery crackers

Directions

Preheat oven to 350°. In a large mixing bowl, combine diced chicken, chopped celery, chopped onion, chopped eggs, toasted almonds, cream of chicken soup, mayonnaise, chicken broth, lemon juice, salt and pepper. Grease a 9 x 13″ baking dish. Spoon chicken mixture into prepared baking dish. Sprinkle crushed crackers over chicken mixture and bake for 40 minutes.

*To toast almonds: Preheat oven to 350°. Spread slivered almonds in a single layer on a baking sheet. Place in preheated oven and bake for 10 to 15 minutes, stirring occasionally.

Divine Chicken Divan

Makes 6 servings

Ingredients

2 (10 oz.) pkgs. frozen broccoli spears

2 C. cooked sliced turkey or chicken

2 (10¾ oz.) cans cream of chicken soup

½ C. mayonnaise

1 tsp. lemon juice

½ tsp. curry powder

½ C. shredded Cheddar cheese

½ C. soft breadcrumbs

1 T. butter, melted

Directions

Preheat oven to 350°. Grease a 7 x 11″ baking dish. In a large saucepan over medium heat, cook broccoli in a small amount of boiling water until crisp-tender; drain. Transfer broccoli to prepared baking dish. Place sliced turkey or chicken over broccoli. In a small bowl, combine cream of chicken soup, mayonnaise, lemon juice and curry powder; mix thoroughly. Pour over mixture in baking dish and sprinkle with shredded Cheddar cheese. In a small bowl, combine breadcrumbs and melted butter; stir well. Spoon breadcrumb mixture over casserole as a topping. Bake for 25 to 30 minutes or until fully heated. Let cool for 5 minutes before serving.

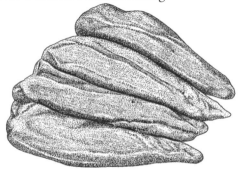

Swiss Almond Chicken Casserole

Makes 8 to10 servings

Ingredients

4 C. cooked chopped chicken

2 C. sliced celery

2 C. herb-seasoned stuffing cubes

1 C. mayonnaise or salad dressing

½ C. milk

¼ C. chopped green onions

1 tsp. salt

Dash of pepper

1 C. shredded Swiss cheese

¼ C. slivered almonds, toasted*

Directions

Preheat oven to 350°. In a large mixing bowl, combine chopped chicken, sliced celery, stuffing cubes, salad dressing, milk, chopped green onions, salt, pepper and Swiss cheese; mix well. Grease the bottom and sides of a 3-quart baking dish and place chicken mixture in dish; sprinkle with toasted almonds. Place lid on casserole dish and bake for 25 minutes. Remove lid and continue baking for 10 additional minutes. Let cool for 5 minutes before serving.

*To toast almonds: Preheat oven to 350°. Spread slivered almonds in a single layer on a baking sheet. Place in preheated oven and bake for 10 to 15 minutes, stirring occasionally.

Oriental Chicken Chow Mein

Makes 4 to 6 servings

Ingredients

2 C. cooked diced chicken

1 (10¾ oz.) can cream of mushroom soup

1 (8 oz.) can pineapple chunks, drained

1 (4 oz.) can sliced mushrooms, drained

1 T. soy sauce

1 C. sliced celery

2 T. chopped green onions

1 (3 oz.) can chow mein noodles, divided

Directions

Preheat oven to 350°. Grease an 8″ square baking dish; set aside. In a medium bowl, combine diced chicken, cream of mushroom soup, pineapple chunks, sliced mushrooms, soy sauce, sliced celery and chopped green onions. Gently stir in 1 cup chow mein noodles and spoon into prepared baking dish. Sprinkle remaining noodles over top. Bake for 45 minutes or until hot and bubbly. Let cool for 5 minutes before serving.

Fiesta Olé

Makes 10 to 12 servings

Ingredients

1 lb. lean ground beef

Salt

Pepper

1 tsp. chili powder

2 C. biscuit baking mix

3 tomatoes, sliced thin

½ C. chopped green
  bell pepper

1 (6 oz.) can sliced black
  olives, drained

1 (8 oz.) pkg. shredded
  Cheddar cheese

1 C. sour cream

⅔ C. mayonnaise

2 T. finely chopped onion

Directions

Preheat oven to 375°. Grease the bottom and sides of a 9 x 13″ baking dish; set aside. In a large skillet over medium heat, brown ground beef until meat is no longer pink; drain well. Add salt and pepper to taste, then stir in chili powder and set aside. In a medium bowl, combine biscuit baking mix and ½ cup water until a soft dough forms. In the prepared baking dish, pat the dough into the bottom and about ½″ up the sides. If the dough is too sticky, flour your hands first. Spread the ground beef inside the dough bowl and layer the sliced tomato, bell pepper and olives in order. In a small bowl, combine Cheddar cheese, sour cream, mayonnaise and chopped onion; stir well. Spoon the cheese mixture evenly over the casserole. Bake for 25 to 30 minutes or until edges of dough are golden brown. Let cool for 5 minutes before serving. Olé!

Home-Baked Taco Casserole

Makes 8 to 10 servings

Ingredients

1 lb. lean ground beef

1 C. chopped onion, divided

1 clove garlic, minced

1 (8 oz.) can tomato sauce

½ C. tomato juice

1 T. chili powder

¼ tsp. oregano

1 (15 oz.) can kidney beans, undrained

1 (8 oz.) pkg. taco-flavored tortilla chips

2 C. shredded lettuce

1 large tomato, chopped

Sour cream, optional

Guacamole, optional

Directions

Preheat oven to 350°. In a large skillet over medium heat, combine ground beef and ½ cup chopped onion. Cook until meat is no longer pink; drain well. Return to stove over medium-low heat and add minced garlic, tomato sauce, tomato juice, chili powder and oregano; simmer for 5 minutes. Grease a 3-quart baking dish. Layer ⅓ of the ground beef mixture, then ⅓ of the kidney beans and top with ⅓ of the tortilla chips. Repeat layers 2 more times. Cover and bake for 35 to 40 minutes or until hot and bubbly. Let cool for 5 minutes. Sprinkle with shredded lettuce, chopped tomato and remaining ½ cup chopped onion. Place a few dollops of sour cream and guacamole on top, if desired.

Burrito Pie

Makes 6 to 8 servings

Ingredients

1 lb. lean ground beef

1 C. biscuit baking mix

1 (16 oz.) can refried beans

1 C. thick salsa

1½ C. shredded
   Cheddar cheese

½ C. sour cream, optional

¼ C. sliced green onions,
   optional

1 tomato, chopped, optional

Directions

Preheat oven to 375°. Grease a 9″ pie plate. In a large skillet over medium heat, brown ground beef until meat is no longer pink; drain well and set aside. In a medium bowl, combine biscuit baking mix with ¼ cup water. Stir in refried beans. Spread evenly into prepared pie plate. Layer cooked ground beef, salsa and shredded cheese in order over dough. Bake for 30 to 35 minutes. Top with sour cream, sliced green onions and chopped tomato, if desired.

Hamburger Hobo Pie

Makes 8 servings

Ingredients

1 lb. lean ground beef

¼ lb. bulk sausage

1 onion, chopped

1 clove garlic, minced

1 (16 oz.) can whole tomatoes, drained and chopped

1 (16 oz.) can whole kernel corn, drained

24 black olives, pitted and sliced

2 tsp. chili powder

1½ tsp. salt

1 C. cornmeal

1 C. milk

2 eggs, beaten

½ C. shredded Cheddar cheese

Fresh parsley sprigs, optional

Directions

Preheat oven to 350°. In a large skillet over medium heat, combine ground beef, sausage, chopped onion and minced garlic. Brown until meat is no longer pink; drain well and set aside. Stir in chopped tomatoes, drained corn, sliced olives, chili powder and salt; heat to boiling. Pour mixture into a greased 2-quart baking dish. In a medium bowl, mix cornmeal, milk and eggs. Pour over meat mixture and sprinkle with Cheddar cheese. Bake for 40 to 50 minutes or until golden brown. Garnish each serving with a sprig of fresh parsley, if desired.

Spiced Cheeseburger Pie

Makes 6 servings

Ingredients

1 lb. lean ground beef

½ C. milk

1 egg

2 cloves garlic, minced

½ tsp. salt

½ tsp. dried oregano

¼ tsp. pepper

½ C. ketchup

½ C. chopped sweet onion

1 (6 oz.) can sliced black olives, drained

1 (12 oz.) pkg. shredded Monterey Jack cheese

2 T. finely chopped fresh parsley

Directions

Preheat oven to 400°. In a large bowl, combine ground beef, milk, egg, minced garlic, salt, oregano and pepper; mix well. Press the mixture evenly into a 9″ pie plate. Layer the ketchup, chopped onions, olives and cheese in order over ingredients in pie plate. Bake for 30 to 35 minutes or until hot and bubbly. Sprinkle with parsley and cut into wedges before serving.

Family Favorite Beef Casserole

Makes 4 to 6 servings

Ingredients

1 C. chopped onion

2 medium potatoes, peeled and sliced

1 lb. lean ground beef

½ C. long grain rice, uncooked

1 C. diced carrots

1 C. diced celery

Salt

Pepper

Paprika

1 (10¾ oz.) can tomato soup

Directions

Preheat oven to 300°. Grease the bottom and sides of a 3-quart baking dish. In dish, layer chopped onions, sliced potatoes, ground beef, uncooked rice, diced carrots and diced celery in order. Sprinkle salt, pepper and paprika between each layer. In a medium bowl, combine 1 cup boiling water with tomato soup; mix thoroughly and pour over the casserole. Bake for 3 hours. Let cool for 5 minutes before serving.

Shrimp & Wild Rice Bake

Makes 8 servings

Ingredients

2½ lbs. shrimp, peeled and deveined

3 (10¾ oz.) cans cream of mushroom soup

1 (6 oz.) box long-grain and wild rice mix

1 large green bell pepper, chopped

1 (2 oz.) jar diced pimentos

1 C. finely chopped onion

1 C. finely chopped celery

1 lb. Cheddar cheese, shredded

Directions

Preheat oven to 350°. Boil, peel and devein the shrimp; set aside. In a large bowl, mix ¾ cup water with cream of mushroom soup; blend well. Cook rice according to package directions. Add shrimp, cooked rice, chopped green bell pepper, pimentos, onion, celery and shredded Cheddar cheese to soup mixture; mix thoroughly. Grease the bottom and sides of a 3-quart baking dish and add shrimp mixture. Bake, uncovered, for 45 to 60 minutes. Serve immediately.

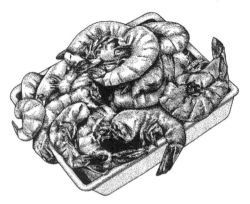

Louisiana-Style Seasoning for Crawfish, Shrimp and Crab

Makes enough for 5 lbs. of seafood

Ingredients

4 T. yellow mustard seeds

3 T. coriander seeds

2 T. whole allspice

2 T. dill seeds

1 tsp. whole cloves

1 T. crushed red pepper

8 bay leaves

Salt

Cayenne pepper

Liquid hot sauce

Directions

In a small bowl, combine mustard seeds, coriander seeds, allspice, dill seeds, cloves, crushed red pepper and bay leaves. Pour into cheesecloth and tie securely with string. When preparing seafood in a large pot of water, add salt, cayenne pepper and hot sauce to taste. Bring to a boil. Add filled cheesecloth bag and boil for several minutes. Liquid should look tinted. Add seafood and cook as directed per item.

Grilled & Barbecued Meats

Picnic Fried Chicken

Makes 16 servings

Ingredients

1½ C. flour

1½ tsp. salt

2 tsp. thyme

2 tsp. paprika

1 egg, beaten

⅓ C. milk

2 T. lemon juice

2 (3 lb.) chicken broilers, cut into pieces

Vegetable oil

Directions

In a shallow dish, combine flour, salt, thyme and paprika. In another shallow dish, combine egg, milk and lemon juice; mix well. Wash chicken pieces but do not dry. Roll chicken pieces in flour mixture, then dip in egg mixture. Roll chicken in flour mixture again; set aside for 30 minutes to allow coating to dry. If coating is still moist, roll in flour again; let dry. In a large skillet over medium-high heat, pour in vegetable oil until it measures ½″ deep. Heat oil to 375°. Place chicken, skin sides down, into the hot oil. Cook for 5 to 10 minutes or until golden brown. Turn over and cook for another 5 to 10 minutes or until golden brown. Reduce heat to medium-low and cover. Cook for 25 minutes or until juices run clear when pierced with a fork. Drain fried chicken on a wire rack or paper towels.

Caribbean Grilled Chicken

Makes 8 servings

Ingredients

1½ C. ketchup

½ C. white wine vinegar

⅓ C. brown sugar

1 T. Worcestershire sauce

2 tsp. grated lime zest

1½ tsp. dry mustard

¾ tsp. garlic powder

½ tsp. salt

¼ tsp. pepper

8 chicken legs

Directions

Place charcoal in an outdoor grill and light the flame. In a small bowl, combine ketchup, vinegar, brown sugar, Worcestershire sauce, lime zest, dry mustard, garlic powder, salt and pepper; mix well. Place chicken legs on grill over medium heat. Occasionally brush chicken with sauce and turn legs often, continuing to brush with remaining sauce as chicken cooks. Grill for 30 to 35 minutes or until juices run clear when chicken is pierced with a fork. Discard marinade.

Garlic Chicken with Lime

Makes 6 servings

Ingredients

6 boneless skinless chicken
   breast halves

⅓ C. soy sauce

¼ C. lime juice

1 T. Worcestershire sauce

½ tsp. dry mustard

2 cloves garlic, minced

½ tsp. pepper

Directions

Place chicken in a large sealable plastic bag or container with lid; set aside. In a small bowl, combine soy sauce, lime juice, Worcestershire sauce, dry mustard and minced garlic; mix well. Pour mixture over chicken and close or cover. Refrigerate for 30 minutes to marinate. Place charcoal in an outdoor grill and light the flame. Remove chicken from container and discard the remaining marinade. Place chicken on grill over medium-low heat, uncovered. Sprinkle with pepper. Turn chicken several times during grilling. Grill for 12 to 15 minutes or until juices run clear when chicken is pierced with a fork.

Quick Marinated Chicken

Makes 4 servings

Ingredients

¼ C. Dijon mustard

2 T. lemon juice

1½ tsp. Worcestershire sauce

½ tsp. dried tarragon

¼ tsp. pepper

4 boneless skinless chicken breast halves

Directions

In a small bowl, combine mustard, lemon juice, Worcestershire sauce, tarragon and pepper; mix well. Spread sauce on both sides of chicken breasts. Marinate at room temperature for 10 to 15 minutes or refrigerate until ready to grill. Place charcoal in an outdoor grill and light the flame. Remove chicken from container and discard the remaining marinade. Place chicken on grill over medium heat, uncovered; turn once during grilling time. Grill for 10 to 15 minutes or until juices run clear when chicken is pierced with a fork.

Pineapple Teriyaki Chicken

Makes 4 servings

Ingredients

1½ C. pineapple juice

½ C. soy sauce

1 tsp. ground ginger

½ tsp. garlic powder

¼ tsp. white pepper

4 boneless skinless chicken breast halves

Directions

In a large bowl, combine pineapple juice, soy sauce, ground ginger, garlic powder and white pepper. If desired, reserve a small amount for dipping sauce while serving. Place chicken in a large sealable plastic bag or container with lid. Pour pineapple mixture over chicken and add enough water to cover. Close or cover container. Refrigerate for 24 hours to marinate. Place charcoal in an outdoor grill and light the flame. Remove chicken from container and discard the remaining marinade. Place chicken on grill over medium-high heat. Grill for 10 to 15 minutes or until juices run clear when chicken is pierced with a fork. Turn chicken once during grilling time. Serve with reserved dipping sauce, if desired.

Baby Back Ribs with Mustard Sauce

Makes 8 servings

Ingredients

⅓ C. brown sugar

¼ C. minced onion

¼ C. white vinegar

¼ C. yellow mustard

½ tsp. celery seed

½ tsp. garlic powder

4 lbs. pork spareribs, separated

Directions

In a medium saucepan, combine brown sugar, minced onion, vinegar, mustard, celery seed and garlic powder. Bring mixture to a boil, stirring until sugar is completely dissolved; set aside. Preheat grill and adjust heat for indirect cooking. Place ribs on grill rack over medium heat; cover and grill for 1 to 1½ hours or until ribs are tender and no pink remains. Brush occasionally with sauce during the last 15 minutes of grilling time.

Pork Loin Beer-B-Que

Makes 12 servings

Ingredients

1 (3 lb.) boneless pork loin

1 (12 oz.) can beer

½ C. dark corn syrup

½ C. finely chopped onion

⅓ C. yellow mustard

¼ C. vegetable oil

2 T. chili powder

2 cloves garlic, minced

Directions

Place pork loin in a shallow glass baking dish; set aside. In a medium bowl, combine beer, corn syrup, chopped onion, mustard, oil, chili powder and minced garlic; mix well. Pour mixture over pork loin, turning the pork loin to coat with marinade. Cover dish with lid or aluminum foil and refrigerate overnight, turning occasionally. Place a drip pan with ½″ of water under an outdoor grill. Bank charcoal in grill and light the flame. Remove pork loin from baking dish. Discard marinade. Grill pork loin over medium-high heat for 1 hour or until a meat thermometer inserted into center of loin reads 145°. Let rest for 10 minutes before slicing. Slice thin to serve.

South-of-the-Border Barbecued Ribs

Makes 4 servings

Ingredients

1 C. ketchup

¼ C. cider vinegar

2 T. Worcestershire sauce

2 tsp. dry mustard

2 tsp. crushed red pepper

½ C. brown sugar

3 to 4 lbs. sparcribs

Directions

In a small saucepan over medium-low heat, combine ketchup, vinegar, Worcestershire sauce, dry mustard, crushed red pepper and brown sugar; heat to boiling. Reduce heat, cover and simmer for 15 minutes. Reserve half of the sauce for serving. Place charcoal in an outdoor grill and light the flame. Place ribs on grill over medium-high heat. Close lid and grill for 10 minutes. Baste with sauce and continue to grill, uncovered. Baste and turn every few minutes. Discard sauce. Grill for an additional 20 minutes or until done. Serve with reserved sauce.

Honey-Orange Barbecued Ribs

Makes 6 servings

Ingredients

3 lbs. country-style ribs

1 (12 oz.) jar chili sauce

½ C. chopped onion

⅓ C. honey

¼ C. butter or margarine

1 clove garlic, minced

¼ tsp. salt

⅛ tsp. hot pepper sauce

¼ tsp. grated orange zest

Directions

Preheat oven to 350°. Using a broiler pan, place ribs on rack and cover with aluminum foil. Roast for 1 hour. In a medium saucepan over medium heat, combine chili sauce, chopped onion, honey, butter, minced garlic, salt and hot pepper sauce; bring to a boil. Reduce heat and cover. Simmer for 30 minutes, then add orange zest. In a small bowl, reserve a little sauce for serving. Remove broiler pan from oven and carefully pour out drippings. Brush sauce over ribs. Roast, uncovered, for 30 minutes. Brush sauce over ribs again. Roast for an additional 20 to 30 minutes or until meat is tender. Serve with reserved sauce and enjoy!

Shrimp Kabobs

Makes 8 servings

Ingredients

2 lbs. jumbo shrimp, peeled and deveined

1 C. Italian salad dressing, divided

2 onions, each cut into 8 wedges

16 large fresh mushrooms

2 large green bell peppers, cut into 1½" pieces

16 cherry tomatoes

Directions

Boil, peel and devein the shrimp. Place shrimp in a large sealable plastic bag or container with lid. Add ½ cup Italian salad dressing to the container with shrimp; set aside. Place onions in a separate large sealable plastic bag or container with lid. Add mushrooms, bell pepper pieces, tomatoes and remaining Italian salad dressing to the container with onions. Seal or cover both containers. Refrigerate for 2 hours, turning shrimp and vegetables occasionally. Place charcoal in an outdoor grill and light the flame. Drain and discard marinade from both containers. Using metal or soaked wooden skewers, thread the shrimp and vegetables alternately onto the skewers. Grill kabobs over medium heat, covered, for 3 minutes. Turn over kabobs and grill for 3 additional minutes or until shrimp turn pink.

Teriyaki Steak Kabobs

Makes 6 servings

Ingredients

1½ lbs. boneless sirloin steak, cut into 1¼" cubes

⅓ C. soy sauce

2 T. vegetable oil

1 T. brown sugar

1 clove garlic, minced

1 tsp. ground ginger

1 tsp. seasoned salt

12 large fresh mushrooms

1 large green bell pepper, cut into 1½" pieces

1 large onion, cut into wedges

12 cherry tomatoes

Directions

Place steak cubes in a large sealable plastic bag or container with lid; set aside. In a medium bowl, combine soy sauce, oil, brown sugar, minced garlic, ground ginger and seasoned salt; mix well. Pour half of the marinade into the container with steak; seal or cover; turn to coat. Pour the remaining marinade into a separate container with lid; cover. Place both containers in refrigerator for 4 to 8 hours, turning steak occasionally. Place charcoal in an outdoor grill and light the flame. Remove both containers from refrigerator. Drain and discard marinade from steak container. Using metal or soaked wooden skewers, thread the steak cubes and vegetables alternately onto the skewers. Grill over medium heat for 3 minutes, uncovered. Turn over kabobs and grill for 3 additional minutes. Brush with reserved marinade. Continue turning and basting for 8 to 10 minutes or until meat is grilled to desired doneness (for rare, 145°; for medium, 160°; for well done, 170°). Discard marinade.

Glazed Sesame Chicken Kabobs

Makes 4 to 6 servings

Ingredients

4 boneless skinless chicken breast halves, cut into 1½" pieces

1 C. vegetable oil

½ C. soy sauce

½ C. light corn syrup

¼ C. lemon juice

2 T. sesame seeds

½ tsp. garlic powder

Garlic salt, to taste

8 large fresh mushrooms

2 onions, quartered

1 green bell pepper, cut into 1½" pieces

Directions

Place chicken pieces in a large sealable plastic bag or container with lid; set aside. In a medium bowl, combine oil, soy sauce, corn syrup, lemon juice, sesame seeds, garlic powder and garlic salt. Pour half of the marinade into the container with chicken; seal or cover. Pour the remaining marinade into a separate container with lid; cover. Place both containers in refrigerator for 4 to 8 hours, turning chicken occasionally. Place charcoal in an outdoor grill and light the flame. Remove both containers from refrigerator. Drain and discard marinade from chicken container. Using metal or soaked wooden skewers, thread chicken pieces and vegetables alternately onto the skewers. Grill over medium heat 8 to 10 minutes. Baste with reserved marinade and continue to grill for 8 to 10 additional minutes, basting frequently. Cook until juices run clear when chicken is pierced with a fork. Discard marinade.

Zesty Almond Chicken Kabobs

Makes 4 servings

Ingredients

4 boneless skinless chicken breast halves, cut into 1½" pieces

1 T. Dijon mustard

1 T. honey

1 T. vegetable oil

1 T. lemon juice

¼ C. chopped almonds, toasted*

Directions

Place chicken pieces in a large sealable plastic bag or container with lid; set aside. In a small bowl, combine mustard, honey, oil and lemon juice. Set aside some of the marinade for basting. Pour remaining marinade into container with chicken; seal or cover. Refrigerate reserved marinade and container with chicken for 1 to 2 hours, turning chicken occasionally. Place charcoal in an outdoor grill and light the flame. Remove containers from refrigerator. Drain and discard the marinade used with the chicken. Thread chicken pieces onto metal or soaked wooden skewers and place on grill. Grill over medium-high heat for 7 to 10 minutes or until juices run clear when chicken is pierced with a fork. Use reserved marinade to baste chicken while grilling. Place toasted almonds in a 10" to 12" plate. When chicken is done, quickly roll kabobs in almonds to coat lightly. Discard marinade.

*To toast almonds: Preheat oven to 350°. Spread chopped almonds in a single layer on a baking sheet. Place in preheated oven and bake for 10 to 15 minutes, stirring occasionally.

West Coast Kabobs

Makes 4 servings

Ingredients

1½ lbs. boneless sirloin steak, cut into 1″ cubes

⅔ C. lemon juice

¼ C. vegetable oil

4 tsp. Worcestershire sauce

2 tsp. paprika

2 cloves garlic, minced

1 tsp. sugar

1 tsp. salt

¼ tsp. hot pepper sauce

16 large fresh mushrooms

2 onions, quartered

2 medium green bell peppers, cut into 1½″ pieces

Directions

Place steak cubes in a large sealable plastic bag or container with lid; set aside. In a medium bowl, combine lemon juice, oil, Worcestershire sauce, paprika, minced garlic, sugar, salt and hot pepper sauce; mix well. Pour ½ cup of marinade over steak in container. Seal or cover container, then turn to coat meat. Pour the remaining marinade into a separate container with lid; cover. Place both containers in refrigerator. Refrigerate for at least 2 hours or overnight, turning steak occasionally. Place charcoal in an outdoor grill and light the flame. Remove both containers from refrigerator. Remove steak from container and discard marinade. Using metal or soaked wooden skewers, thread the steak cubes and vegetables alternately onto skewers. Place kabobs on grill. Use reserved marinade to baste steak while grilling. Grill over medium heat for 8 to 10 minutes or until meat is grilled to desired doneness (for rare, 145°; for medium, 160°; for well done, 170°). Discard the remaining marinade.

Grilled Turkey with Red Wine

Makes 12 to 16 servings

Ingredients

1 (12 lb.) whole turkey
1 onion, diced
Salt

Pepper
1 (750 ml.) bottle red wine

Directions

Place charcoal in an outdoor grill and light the flame. Remove neck and giblets from turkey; discard. Clean turkey and pat dry. Stuff turkey with diced onion and rub the exterior with salt and pepper. Place turkey in an aluminum roasting pan. Reserve ½ cup wine for basting. Pour the remaining wine over turkey. Loosely cover turkey with aluminum foil. Close lid on grill and open the vents. Grill for 2 to 3 hours over medium-low heat or until a meat thermometer reads 165°, as measured in the innermost part of the thigh. Baste frequently with reserved red wine. Water may be added if wine evaporates too quickly.

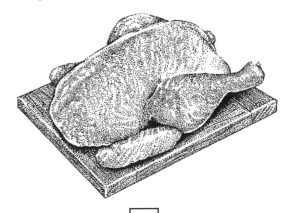

Honey Smoked Turkey

Makes 12 to 16 servings

Ingredients

½ lb. mesquite wood chips for charcoal

1 (12 lb.) whole turkey

2 T. chopped fresh sage

2 T. pepper

2 T. celery salt

2 T. chopped fresh basil

2 T. vegetable oil

1 (12 oz.) jar honey

Directions

Preheat grill to medium-high heat. If you are using an outdoor charcoal grill, use twice the amount of charcoal you would normally use. Soak wood chips in a pan of water; set to the side of grill. Remove neck and giblets from turkey; discard. Clean turkey and pat dry. Place turkey in an aluminum roasting pan; set aside. In a small bowl, combine sage, pepper, celery salt, basil and oil. Pour mixture evenly over turkey. Turn the turkey breast side down in the pan. Loosely cover turkey with aluminum foil. Place pan on grill. Throw a handful of the wood chips on the fire. Close lid and grill for 1 hour. Throw 2 more handfuls of wood chips on the fire. Drizzle half of the honey over the turkey and replace the aluminum foil. Close the lid and continue to grill for 1½ to 2 hours or until a meat thermometer reads 165°, as measured in the innermost part of the thigh. Uncover turkey and turn it breast side up. Baste with remaining honey. Leave uncovered and grill for 15 minutes longer. The honey will give the turkey skin a very dark golden color.

Tuscan Grilled Steak

Makes 4 servings

Ingredients

3 cloves garlic, crushed

1 (2 lb.) flank steak

Salt

Pepper

2 tsp. olive oil

Directions

Place charcoal in an outdoor grill and light the flame. In a small bowl, mash garlic cloves into a paste. Pat steaks dry with a paper towel. Sprinkle with salt and pepper. Rub garlic paste on both sides of steak and let it rest for 30 minutes. Place steak on grill over high heat. Grill for 5 to 7 minutes on one side. Meat should be well-seared and brown. Turn steak over and grill for 3 to 5 minutes or until meat is medium rare. To test, cut steak with a knife; meat should be almost to your preferred doneness. Transfer steak to a cutting board and cover loosely with aluminum foil. Let steak rest for 10 minutes, as it will continue to cook after it is removed from the heat. Cut the steak into very thin slices against the grain at a slight angle.

Balsamic Marinated Flank Steak

Makes 6 servings

Ingredients

1 red onion, quartered

⅓ C. balsamic vinegar

¼ C. capers, drained

2 T. chopped fresh oregano

3 cloves garlic, minced

¼ tsp. salt

¼ tsp. pepper

1½ lbs. flank steak

Directions

Sliver one quarter of the onion and place it in a bowl; cover and set aside. Chop the remaining onion sections. In a medium bowl, combine chopped onion, vinegar, capers, oregano and minced garlic. Add ¼ of this mixture to the slivered onions; cover and set aside. Sprinkle salt and pepper over both sides of the steak. Using a fork, pierce holes into surface of steak. Place steak in a large sealable plastic bag or container with lid. Add the remaining chopped onion mixture. Place both containers in refrigerator. Marinate steak for 1 hour or overnight, turning occasionally. Remove steak container from refrigerator. Place steak on grill over direct heat; discard marinade. If using an oven broiler, position broiler rack so meat will be 4″ from heat source. Grill for 3 to 4 minutes. Turn steaks over and grill for 3 to 4 additional minutes or until meat is cooked to desired doneness (for rare, 145°; for medium, 160°; for well done, 170°). Let stand for 5 minutes before slicing. Remove slivered onion mixture from refrigerator. Place meat on a platter and pour the reserved onion mixture over steak.

Grilled Delmonico Steak

Makes 4 servings

Ingredients

½ C. olive oil

¼ C. Worcestershire sauce

6 T. soy sauce

¼ C. minced garlic

¾ C. chopped onion

2 T. salt

1 T. pepper

1 T. dried rosemary

3 T. steak seasoning, any kind

3 T. steak sauce, any kind

4 (10 oz.) ribeye steaks

Directions

In a blender or food processor, combine olive oil, Worcestershire sauce, soy sauce, minced garlic, chopped onion, salt, pepper, rosemary, steak seasoning and steak sauce. Process until well blended. Using a fork, pierce holes into surface of steak. Place steak in a large sealable plastic bag or container with lid. Pour marinade over steaks and cover. Place container in refrigerator to marinate steaks for 3 hours or overnight, turning occasionally. Place charcoal in an outdoor grill and light the flame. Remove steak container from refrigerator. Place steaks on grill over medium heat; discard marinade. Grill for 8 to 10 minutes. Turn over and grill for 8 to 10 additional minutes or until meat is cooked to desired doneness (for rare, 145°; for medium, 160°; for well done, 170°).

Cilantro Grilled Halibut

Makes 4 servings

Ingredients

1 lime, cut into 4 wedges

4 (6 oz.) halibut fillets

Salt

Pepper

1 T. olive oil

3 cloves garlic, minced

2 T. butter

½ C. chopped fresh cilantro

Directions

Place charcoal in an outdoor grill and light the flame. Reserve 1 wedge of lime for later use. Squeeze the juice from the remaining 3 lime wedges over fillets and season with salt and pepper. Grill fillets over high heat for 5 minutes. Turn over and grill for 5 additional minutes or until fish flakes easily with a fork. In a large skillet over medium heat, heat oil. Add minced garlic; cook and stir until fragrant, about 2 minutes. Add butter, lime juice from remaining lime wedge and cilantro. Be sure to remove any stray lime seeds. Remove from heat and serve butter sauce drizzled over fish.

Easy Grilled Salmon

Makes 6 servings

Ingredients

1½ lbs. salmon fillets

Lemon pepper

Garlic powder

Salt

⅓ C. soy sauce

⅓ C. brown sugar

¼ C. vegetable oil

Directions

Season salmon fillets to taste with lemon pepper, garlic powder and salt. In a small bowl, combine soy sauce, brown sugar, oil and ⅓ cup water. Place seasoned fillets in a large sealable plastic bag. Add soy sauce mixture and seal bag tightly. Place bag in refrigerator to marinate salmon for at least 2 hours, turning frequently. Preheat grill to medium heat and lightly oil the grate. Place salmon on the preheated grill, skin side down. Discard the marinade. Cook salmon for about 10 minutes without turning. Fish is done when it flakes easily with a fork.

Quick Juicy Burgers

Makes 8 servings

Ingredients

2 lbs. lean ground beef

1 egg, beaten

¾ C. dry breadcrumbs

3 T. evaporated milk

2 T. Worcestershire sauce

2 cloves garlic, minced

⅛ tsp. cayenne pepper

Salt, optional

Pepper, optional

8 hamburger buns

Directions

Preheat the grill to high heat and lightly oil the grate. In a large bowl, mix ground beef, beaten egg, dry breadcrumbs, evaporated milk, Worcestershire sauce, minced garlic and cayenne pepper by hand until well blended. Form the mixture into 8 patties. Place patties on the prepared grill and cook for 5 minutes on each side or until internal temperature of burgers reaches 160° on a meat thermometer. Season burgers with salt and pepper to taste, if desired. Serve patties on hamburger buns.

Tasty Barbecued Burgers

Makes 4 servings

Ingredients

1 lb. lean ground beef

1 egg, beaten

¼ C. uncooked oats

1 T. dried onion flakes

1 tsp. dry onion soup mix

½ tsp. seasoned salt

Dash of pepper

2 T. ketchup

4 hamburger buns

Directions

Preheat the grill to high heat and lightly oil the grate. In a large bowl, mix ground beef, beaten egg, oats, onion flakes, onion soup mix, seasoned salt, pepper and ketchup by hand until well blended. Form the mixture into 4 patties. Place patties on the prepared grill and cook for 5 minutes on each side or until internal temperature of burgers reaches 160° on a meat thermometer. Serve patties on hamburger buns.

Bacon Mushroom Burgers

Makes 4 to 5 servings

Ingredients

1 (4 oz.) can mushrooms, drained

1 lb. lean ground beef

4 bacon strips, cooked and crumbled

2 T. diced green onions

1 tsp. Worcestershire sauce

1 tsp. soy sauce

½ tsp. salt

4 to 5 hamburger buns

Tomato slices, optional

Directions

Preheat the grill to high heat and lightly oil the grate. Cut the drained mushrooms into small pieces. In a large bowl, mix mushroom pieces, ground beef, crumbled bacon, diced green onions, Worcestershire sauce, soy sauce and salt until well blended. Form mixture into 4 or 5 patties. Place patties on the prepared grill and cook for 5 to 6 minutes on each side or until internal temperature of burgers reaches 160° on a meat thermometer. Serve patties on hamburger buns. If desired, top each burger with a few tomato slices.

Saucy Calico Burgers

Makes 4 to 6 servings

Ingredients

1½ lbs. lean ground beef

½ C. cooked rice

¼ C. chopped onion

¼ C. chopped green
bell pepper

1 T. dried parsley flakes

1 tsp. salt

¼ tsp. garlic powder

Dash of pepper

¼ C. ketchup

3 T. chili sauce

1 tsp. Worcestershire sauce

¼ tsp. dried basil

4 to 6 hamburger buns,
optional

Directions

Preheat the grill to high heat and lightly oil the grate. In a large bowl, mix ground beef, cooked rice, chopped onion, chopped green pepper, parsley flakes, salt, garlic powder and pepper by hand until well blended. Form mixture into 4 to 6 oval patties. Place patties on the prepared grill and cook for 7 to 10 minutes on each side or until internal temperature reaches 160° on a meat thermometer. To prepare barbecue sauce, in a small saucepan, place ⅔ cup water, ketchup, chili sauce, Worcestershire sauce and basil. Simmer over low heat for 15 minutes, stirring occasionally. Serve sauce over burgers, with or without buns.

Delicious Grilled Bratwurst

Makes 5 to 6 servings

Ingredients

5 fresh bratwurst sausages

1 medium onion, thinly sliced

½ C. butter, optional

3 (12 oz.) cans or bottles beer

¾ tsp. pepper

½ tsp. celery seed, optional

5 to 6 hoagie rolls

Directions

In a large saucepan over medium-low heat, place bratwurst sausages, sliced onions, butter, beer, pepper and celery seed. Simmer slowly for about 20 minutes. Preheat grill to medium-high heat and lightly oil the grill grate. Cook bratwurst on grill for 10 to 14 minutes, turning occasionally to brown evenly. Be careful not to overcook. Serve cooked bratwurst hot off the grill on hoagie rolls. Add a few onion slices from saucepan to each hoagie roll. If unable to serve immediately, place the grilled bratwurst back into the beer brine and simmer over low heat until ready to serve.

Spicy Grilled Bratwurst

Makes 6 servings

Ingredients

1 (12 oz.) can or bottle beer

2 T. brown sugar

2 T. soy sauce

1 T. yellow mustard

1 tsp. chili powder

2 cloves garlic, minced

2 to 3 drops hot pepper sauce

6 fresh bratwurst sausages

6 hoagie rolls

Sauerkraut relish, optional

Directions

In a large skillet over low heat, combine beer, brown sugar, soy sauce, mustard, chili powder, minced garlic and hot pepper sauce; mix well. Add bratwurst sausages to marinade and simmer over low heat for 20 minutes. Preheat grill to medium heat and lightly oil the grate. Remove bratwurst from marinade and place on grill. Cook bratwurst for 10 to 14 minutes, turning occasionally to brown evenly. Meanwhile, keep the marinade warm over the stovetop. Serve cooked bratwurst on hoagie rolls. Garnish with sauerkraut relish, if desired. If unable to serve immediately, place the grilled bratwurst back into the marinade and keep warm over low heat until ready to serve.

Desserts

Raspberry Peach Cobbler

Makes 8 servings

Ingredients

2 C. fresh raspberries

2½ C. sliced fresh peaches

½ C. sugar

1 T. cornstarch

1 tsp. nutmeg

2 C. biscuit baking mix

½ C. milk

3 T. butter, melted

2 T. brown sugar

Directions

Preheat oven to 375°. Lightly grease bottom and sides of a 9″ pie plate. In a large bowl, combine raspberries, peaches, sugar, cornstarch and nutmeg. Let stand for 10 minutes, then spoon into pie plate. Using the same bowl, stir together biscuit baking mix, milk, melted butter and brown sugar to make a dough. Drop dough by spoonfuls over fruit mixture in pie plate. Bake for 25 to 30 minutes or until fruit is bubbly and topping is deep golden brown.

Strawberry Rhubarb Cobbler

Makes 8 servings

Ingredients

1 lb. rhubarb, chopped

⅔ C. plus 3 T. sugar, divided

1 C. plus 1 T. flour, divided

1½ C. sliced strawberries

1½ tsp. baking powder

Pinch of salt

4 T. butter or margarine, cold

½ C. half-and-half

Directions

Preheat oven to 400°. Lightly grease bottom and sides of a 7 x 11″ baking dish. In a large bowl, toss together chopped rhubarb, ⅔ cup sugar and 1 tablespoon flour. Pour mixture into baking dish and bake for approximately 7 minutes. Meanwhile, prepare cobbler dough. In a medium bowl, mix remaining 1 cup flour, remaining 3 tablespoons sugar, baking powder and salt. Cut in butter using a pastry blender and stir in half-and-half. Remove baking dish from oven. Spread sliced strawberries over rhubarb and drop dough by spoonfuls on top. Bake for 20 to 25 minutes or until fruit is bubbly and topping is deep golden brown.

Very Cherry Cobbler

Makes 8 Servings

Ingredients

½ C. butter

1 C. flour

1 tsp. baking powder

½ tsp. salt

1 C. milk

1 C. sugar

1 (32 oz.) can cherry pie filling

Directions

Preheat oven to 350°. Place butter in a 9 x 13″ baking dish; set dish in oven until butter is melted. In a medium bowl, combine flour, baking powder, salt, milk and sugar. Transfer flour mixture to baking dish with melted butter and spread evenly. Spread cherry pie filling evenly over crumb layer. Bake for 45 to 60 minutes or until fruit is bubbly.

Apple Cinnamon Brown Betty

Makes 8 servings

Ingredients

6 bread slices, toasted and cubed

1 C. sugar

2 tsp. cinnamon

6 baking apples, peeled, cored and sliced

½ C. butter or margarine, melted

1 C. orange juice

Directions

Preheat oven to 350°. Divide toast cubes into 4 equal portions. In a small bowl, combine sugar and cinnamon; set aside. Grease a 7 x 11″ baking dish. Layer one portion of the toast cubes across the bottom of dish and drizzle with ⅓ of the melted butter. Layer ⅓ of the sliced apples on top and sprinkle with ⅓ of the sugar-cinnamon mixture. Drizzle with ⅓ cup orange juice. Repeat layers 2 more times, ending with a toast layer. Bake for 20 to 30 minutes or until fruit is bubbly. Serve warm with a scoop of vanilla ice cream.

Delicious Four Fruit Pizza

Makes 12 servings

Ingredients

1 (18 oz.) pkg. refrigerated sugar cookie dough

1 (8 oz.) carton whipped topping

½ C. sliced banana

½ C. sliced strawberries

½ C. crushed pineapple, drained

½ C. seedless grapes, halved

Directions

Preheat oven to 350°. Press cookie dough evenly into a 12″ pizza pan. Bake for 15 to 20 minutes or until golden brown. After removing from oven, place pan on a wire rack to cool completely. Spread whipped topping evenly over crust. Place fruit on whipped topping in your favorite design or in broad to small circles. Refrigerate until ready to serve.

Chocolate Butter Brickle Bars

Makes 36 servings

Ingredients

1 (18½ oz.) box butter brickle cake mix

2 eggs

¼ C. butter or margarine

¼ C. brown sugar

¾ C. chopped nuts

1 (6 oz.) pkg. chocolate chips

1 (16 oz.) can chocolate frosting

Directions

Preheat oven to 350°. In a large bowl, combine cake mix, ¼ cup water, eggs, butter and brown sugar; mix well. Stir in chopped nuts and chocolate chips. Bake for 20 to 25 minutes or until golden brown. When cool, top bars with chocolate frosting.

Choco-Toffee Bars

Makes 24 servings

Ingredients

1 (18 oz.) pkg. refrigerated chocolate chip cookie dough

1 (14 oz.) can sweetened condensed milk

1 C. almond toffee bits

1 C. shredded coconut, divided

½ C. sliced almonds, divided

1 C. semi-sweet chocolate chips

Directions

Preheat oven to 350°. Line a 9 x 13″ baking pan with non-stick aluminum foil, dull side up, extending foil up and over the sides of the pan. Press cookie dough across the bottom of the foil-lined pan to make the crust. Bake for 15 to 17 minutes or until crust is lightly browned. In a medium bowl, combine sweetened condensed milk, toffee bits, ½ cup shredded coconut and ¼ cup sliced almonds; stir. Spread mixture evenly over hot baked crust. Sprinkle chocolate chips and remaining coconut and almonds on top. Bake for 20 to 25 minutes or until coconut is light golden brown. Cool completely and lift foil to remove from pan. Cut into bars and serve.

Pecan Graham Crunchies

Make 12 servings

Ingredients

8 whole graham crackers

1 C. chopped pecans

1 C. butter

½ C. sugar

Directions

Preheat oven to 350°. Line a 9 x 13″ baking dish with aluminum foil. Place graham crackers flat inside pan, dividing as needed to cover bottom of pan in one layer. Sprinkle chopped pecans over crackers. In a small saucepan over medium heat, place butter and sugar. Bring to a boil for 4 minutes, stirring until sugar is completely dissolved. Remove saucepan from heat and pour hot liquid over pecan layer, covering completely. Place baking dish in oven for 10 minutes. Remove from oven and let cool completely before peeling crackers from aluminum foil. Break into pieces and store in an airtight container.

Simple Macaroons

Makes 36 servings

Ingredients

3 egg whites

¼ tsp. salt

½ tsp. lemon juice

½ C. sugar

2½ C. shredded coconut

Directions

Preheat oven to 350°. In a medium bowl, beat egg whites with salt and lemon juice until foamy. Gradually add sugar and continue to beat until thick and stiff. Fold in shredded coconut. Drop dough by teaspoonfuls onto a greased baking sheet and bake for 15 minutes or until macaroons are golden.

Strawberry Gelatin Pineapple Surprise

Makes 20 servings

Ingredients

2 C. crushed unsalted pretzels

3 T. plus 1 C. sugar, divided

¾ C. butter or margarine, melted

1 (8 oz.) pkg. cream cheese, softened

1 (8 oz.) carton whipped topping

1 (6 oz.) pkg. strawberry gelatin mix

2 (10 oz.) pkgs. frozen strawberries, thawed

1 (8 oz.) can crushed pineapple, drained

Directions

Preheat oven to 400°. In a small bowl, combine crushed pretzels, 3 tablespoons sugar and melted butter. Spread mixture evenly across bottom of a 9 x 13″ baking dish. Bake for 7 minutes. Remove from oven and set aside to cool for 1 hour. In a medium bowl, blend together cream cheese, remaining 1 cup sugar and whipped topping. Spread on top of cooled pretzel layer; set aside. In a small saucepan, bring 2 cups water to a boil. Remove from heat and pour water into a medium bowl. Stir in strawberry gelatin, mixing until dissolved. Stir in strawberries and pineapple; chill in refrigerator until just partially jelled. Spread on top of cream cheese mixture in baking dish. Chill until gelatin layer is firm. Cut into pieces and serve.

Texas Sheet Cake

Makes 24 servings

Ingredients

1 C. hot brewed coffee

1½ C. butter, divided

6 T. plus 5 T. unsweetened cocoa powder, divided

2 C. flour

2 C. sugar

1 tsp. baking soda

½ tsp. salt

3 eggs

1 (8 oz.) container sour cream

2 tsp. vanilla, divided

6 T. milk

4 C. powdered sugar

1 C. chopped pecans, optional

Directions

Preheat oven to 350°. Grease and flour a 12 x 18″ sheet pan. In a medium saucepan over medium heat, combine coffee, 1 cup butter and 5 tablespoons unsweetened cocoa powder. Bring mixture to a boil, reduce heat and stir until smooth. Remove from heat and set aside. In a large bowl, combine flour, sugar, baking soda and salt. Form a well in the center of the mixture and add eggs, sour cream and 1 teaspoon vanilla. Mix well, then beat in coffee mixture. Spread batter into prepared sheet pan. Bake for 20 to 25 minutes, or until a toothpick inserted into the center of the cake comes out clean. Meanwhile, prepare frosting. Cake should be frosted while it is still warm. In a medium saucepan over medium heat, combine remaining ½ cup butter, milk and remaining 6 tablespoons unsweetened cocoa powder; stir until smooth. Remove from heat and mix in powdered sugar, stirring until frosting is smooth. If frosting is too thick, add a little more milk. Stir in remaining 1 teaspoon vanilla and chopped pecans; spread over warm cake.

Sunflower Dirt Cake

Makes 8 to 10 servings

Ingredients

4 T. butter, softened

1 (8 oz.) pkg. cream cheese, softened

1 C. powdered sugar

2 (3½ oz.) boxes instant vanilla pudding mix

3½ C. milk

1 (12 oz.) carton whipped topping

2 (20 oz.) pkgs. cream-filled chocolate sandwich cookies

12 gummy worms

1 (10″) clay flower pot

1 plastic sunflower with a long stem

Plastic shovel

Directions

In a large bowl, combine butter, cream cheese and powdered sugar. Mix until thoroughly blended. In a medium bowl, combine vanilla pudding mix and milk; stir in whipped topping. Add pudding mixture to cream cheese mixture; stir well. Crush the cream-filled chocolate sandwich cookies into fine crumbs. Line the inside of a 10″ clay flower pot with heavy-duty aluminum foil. Place one layer of cookie crumbs across bottom of the flower pot, then top with a layer of cream filling. Repeat layers a few more times ending with a layer of cookie crumbs. Top with gummy worms. Wash the plastic flower and stem and let dry. Place the plastic sunflower stem into the center of the cake as decoration. Use a clean plastic shovel for the "scoop".

No-Egg Chocolate Cake

Makes 24 servings

Ingredients

1½ C. flour

⅓ C. sweetened cocoa powder

1 tsp. baking soda

½ tsp. salt

1 C. sugar

½ C. vegetable oil

2 tsp. vanilla

2 tsp. vinegar

Directions

Preheat oven to 375°. Spray an 8 x 12″ baking dish with non-stick vegetable spray. In a medium bowl, combine flour, cocoa powder, baking soda, salt and sugar; mix well. Pour mixture into prepared baking dish. Using the same bowl, mix oil, 1 cup cold water and vanilla. Add liquid mixture to baking pan and mix thoroughly. Quickly stir in vinegar and spread evenly. Bake for 25 to 30 minutes. Cool before cutting into pieces.

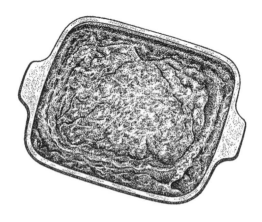

Applesauce Cake with Streusel Topping

Makes 24 servings

Ingredients

1 C. plus 2 T. butter, divided

3½ C. applesauce

4¼ C. flour, divided

2½ C. sugar, divided

2 tsp. salt

2 tsp. baking soda

2¼ tsp. cinnamon, divided

½ tsp. allspice

1 tsp. nutmeg

2 C. chopped walnuts

¼ C. crushed corn flake cereal

Directions

Preheat oven to 350°. Grease the bottom of an 8 x 12″ baking dish. In a large saucepan over medium heat, combine 1 cup butter and applesauce until butter is melted, stirring occasionally. Remove from heat. In a medium bowl, combine 4 cups sifted flour, 2 cups sugar, salt, baking soda, 2 teaspoons cinnamon, allspice and nutmeg. Add dry mixture to butter mixture and mix thoroughly; stir in chopped walnuts. Pour batter into prepared pan, spread evenly and set aside. In a small bowl, combine remaining ¼ cup flour, remaining ½ cup sugar, crushed corn flake cereal and remaining ¼ teaspoon cinnamon. Using a pastry blender, cut in remaining 2 tablespoons butter until mixture is crumbly. Sprinkle on top of prepared cake batter. Bake for 40 to 45 minutes or until a toothpick inserted into the center of the cake comes out clean.

Easy Flag Cake

Makes 12 servings

Ingredients

1 (17¾ oz.) box white or
   yellow cake mix

2 pints fresh strawberries,
   divided

1⅓ C. fresh blueberries,
   divided

1 (12 oz.) carton whipped
   topping

Directions

Prepare cake according to package directions for a 9 x 13″ baking dish. After baking, cool cake completely. Slice 1 cup of strawberries. Cut remaining strawberries into halves. Cover cake in pan with sliced strawberries and 1 cup blueberries. Spread whipped topping evenly over berries on cake. Arrange remaining strawberry halves and blueberries over the whipped topping to create a 'stars and stripes' flag design. Refrigerate until ready to serve.

Fun-in-the-Sun Cake

Makes 14 servings

Ingredients

1½ C. butter, softened

2 C. sugar

4 eggs

½ tsp. salt

2 tsp. baking soda

1 (20 oz.) can crushed pineapple

¼ C. unsweetened pineapple juice

1 (3½ oz.) pkg. shredded coconut

1 C. chopped walnuts

2 tsp. vanilla

1 (16 oz.) pkg. graham crackers, crushed

1 (8 oz.) carton whipped topping, optional

Directions

Preheat oven to 350°. Grease a 10″ tube pan and line it with parchment paper. In a medium bowl, cream together butter, sugar and eggs. Add salt, baking soda, crushed pineapple and pineapple juice; mix well. Add shredded coconut, chopped walnuts and vanilla. Mix in graham cracker crumbs. Pour mixture into prepared pan and bake for 90 minutes or until top springs back when lightly touched. Top each serving with a dollop of whipped topping, as desired.

Heavenly Strawberry Dessert

Makes 18 servings

Ingredients

2 (8 oz.) pkgs. cream cheese, softened

1 C. sugar

1 (8 oz.) carton whipped topping

1 (10") prepared angel food cake

1 qt. fresh strawberries, sliced

1 (18 oz.) jar strawberry glaze

Directions

In a medium bowl, combine cream cheese and sugar until light and fluffy. Fold in whipped topping and set aside. Tear the angel food cake into small pieces and place in the bottom of a 9 x 13" baking dish. Using a piece of plastic wrap or parchment paper, press the cake pieces down into the baking dish. Spread the whipped topping mixture over cake layer. In a separate bowl, combine sliced strawberries and glaze, mixing until strawberries are evenly coated. Spread glazed strawberries over whipped topping mixture on cake. Refrigerate for 2 hours or until ready to serve.

Sin-sational
Strawberry Shortcake

Makes 9 servings

Ingredients

3 pints fresh strawberries, sliced

½ C. plus 2 T. sugar, divided

2¼ C. flour

4 tsp. baking powder

¼ tsp. salt

⅓ C. shortening

1 egg, beaten

⅔ C. milk

1 (8 oz.) carton whipped topping

Directions

Preheat oven to 425°. Toss sliced strawberries in ½ cup sugar; set aside. Grease and flour an 8″ round cake pan. In a medium bowl, combine flour, baking powder, remaining 2 tablespoons sugar and salt. Using a pastry blender, cut in shortening until mixture is crumbly. Form a well in the center of the flour mixture; add beaten egg and milk. Stir until combined and spread batter in pan. Bake for 15 to 20 minutes or until golden brown. Remove from oven and let cool on a wire rack, approximately 20 minutes. Remove cake from pan and slice partially cooled cake in half horizontally. Place bottom half on cake platter and cover with half of the sugar-coated strawberries. Place the top half of cake on top and cover with remaining strawberries. Spread whipped topping over top and sides of cake.

No-Bake Frozen Peanut Butter Pie

Makes 2 (9″) pies

Ingredients

1 (8 oz.) pkg. cream cheese, softened

1½ C. powdered sugar

1 C. peanut butter

1 C. milk

1 (16 oz.) carton whipped topping

2 (9″) prepared graham cracker pie crusts

16 mint leaves, optional

Directions

In a large bowl, combine cream cheese and powdered sugar; mix well. Add peanut butter and milk; beat until smooth. Fold in whipped topping. Transfer half of the mixture into one graham cracker crust and the other half into the remaining graham cracker crust. Cover pies with plastic wrap and freeze until mixture is firm. Slice each pie into 8 pieces. Decorate each slice with a mint leaf, if desired.

Key Lime Pretzel Surprise

Makes 8 servings

Ingredients

⅓ C. butter

3 T. sugar

1¼ C. crushed pretzels

¼ C. key lime juice

1 (14 oz.) can sweetened condensed milk

1 (8 oz.) carton whipped topping

Directions

Preheat oven to 350°. In a small saucepan over medium-low heat, melt butter and then mix in sugar. Remove from stovetop and add crushed pretzels; mix well. Spray a 9″ pie plate with non-stick vegetable spray. Transfer pretzel mixture into pie plate. Use a piece of plastic wrap or parchment paper to press the mixture into the pan to form the crust. Bake for 7 to 9 minutes. Remove from oven and cool completely before continuing. In a medium bowl, combine key lime juice and sweetened condensed milk; mix well. Pour lime mixture into prepared crust and refrigerate overnight. To serve, top each slice with a dollop of whipped topping or use a pastry bag to pipe the whipped topping over the whole pie.

Marvelous Lemonade Pie

Makes 8 servings

Ingredients

1 (6 oz.) can frozen lemonade concentrate, thawed

1 (14 oz.) can sweetened condensed milk

1 (8 oz.) carton whipped topping

1 (9″) prepared graham cracker pie crust

Directions

In a large bowl, combine lemonade concentrate and sweetened condensed milk; mix well. Fold in whipped topping. Transfer mixture into prepared graham cracker crust; spread evenly. Refrigerate for 2 hours or until ready to serve.

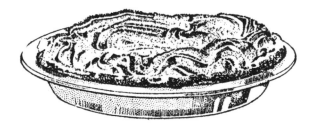

Cinnamon Raisin Pie

Makes 8 servings

Ingredients

2 C. raisins

½ C. brown sugar

2 T. cornstarch

½ tsp. cinnamon

¼ tsp. salt

1 T. white vinegar

1 T. butter or margarine

Pastry for 2-crust pie

Directions

Preheat oven to 425°. In a small saucepan over medium-high heat, combine raisins and 2 cups water; bring to a boil for 5 minutes, stirring often. Meanwhile, in a small bowl, combine brown sugar, cornstarch, cinnamon and salt; stir. Add brown sugar mixture to raisins and boiling water. Cook and stir over medium heat until syrup becomes clear. Remove from heat and stir in vinegar and butter; cool slightly. Line a 9″ pie plate with one pastry layer and trim off edges as needed. Pour filling into pie crust. Cover with remaining pastry and seal edges. Using a sharp knife, cut slits in top crust. Bake for 30 to 35 minutes or until crust is golden brown. Serve warm or cooled.

Amazing Apple Pie

Makes 8 servings

Ingredients

1 C. sugar

1 tsp. cinnamon

Dash of nutmeg

1 T. cornstarch

Dash of salt

7 tart apples, peeled, cored and sliced, or 5 C. frozen apple slices

Pastry for 2-crust pie

2 T. butter

Directions

Preheat oven to 400°. In a large bowl, combine sugar, cinnamon, nutmeg, cornstarch and salt. Add sliced apples and mix well. Line a 9″ pie plate with one pastry layer and trim off edges as needed. Transfer apple mixture into pie crust and dot with pieces of butter. Cover with remaining pastry and seal edges. Sprinkle a little sugar over top crust. Using a sharp knife, cut slits in an apple shape in top crust. Bake for 50 minutes or until crust is golden brown.

Cinnamon Peach Pie

Makes 8 servings

Ingredients

2 (16 oz.) cans sliced peaches

½ C. sugar

2 T. flour

¼ tsp. nutmeg

Pinch of salt

2 T. butter or margarine

1 T. fresh lemon juice

Pastry for 2-crust pie

Cinnamon and sugar mixture

8 mint sprigs, optional

Vanilla ice cream, optional

Directions

Preheat oven to 400°. Drain peaches, reserving ⅓ cup syrup. Save the remaining syrup as a pie topping, if desired. In a large saucepan over medium heat, combine sugar, flour, nutmeg and salt. Add reserved ⅓ cup peach syrup and cook, stirring continually, until mixture becomes thick and bubbly. Add butter, lemon juice and sliced peaches. Remove from heat; let cool. Line a 9″ pie plate with one pastry layer and trim off edges as needed. Transfer peach mixture into pie crust. Cut lattice strips, ½″ wide, out of the remaining pastry by using a wavy edged pastry wheel. Put lattice on top of pie resembling a woven basket, leaving ½″ between each section. Sprinkle top with cinnamon and sugar mixture. Bake for 40 to 45 minutes or until golden brown. Garnish with mint sprigs or serve with vanilla ice cream and additional peach syrup, if desired.

Basic Single Pie Crust

Makes 1 (8″ or 9″) pie crust

Ingredients

1 C. flour

½ tsp. salt

⅓ C. plus 1 T. shortening

Directions

Preheat oven to 425°. In a medium bowl, combine flour and salt. Cut shortening into mixture until particles are the size of small peas. Sprinkle with ice cold water, 1 tablespoon at a time, tossing with a fork to make sure not to over-moisten. Generally 2 tablespoons of water is enough. Use a fork to stir until all flour is moistened and pastry almost forms together off the side of bowl. Using both hands, gently form a ball of dough and place it on a lightly floured surface. With a floured rolling pin, roll out the dough from the center to form a 12″ circle. To transfer dough to pie pan, fold it in quarters, then place point in center of pie pan and unfold. Crimp crust edge, then poke holes in the bottom with a fork to prevent bubbling*. Bake for 15 minutes or until crust is golden brown. Cool before filling.

*Note: If pie crust needs to be baked after being filled, do not poke holes in the bottom crust.

To Make a Double Pie Crust

Make 2 (8″ or 9″) pie crusts

Double the ingredients and follow the directions above. Divide dough into 2 balls before rolling it out.

Index

Finger Foods

Salads

Index

Casseroles & Deep Dishes

Index

Grilled & Barbecued Meats

Index

Desserts